# conten

G000274121

# minced meat

## moroccan tart

1 sheet ready-rolled shortcrust pastry
1 tablespoon olive oil
300g (9½ ounces) minced (ground) lamb
1 teaspoon ground coriander
½ teaspoon ground cinnamon
400g (12½ ounces) canned chickpeas (garbanzo),
  rinsed, drained
1 clove garlic, crushed
2 tablespoons lemon juice
1 piece preserved lemon rind (30g), trimmed,
  chopped finely
2 tablespoons roasted pine nuts
125g (4 ounces) fetta cheese, crumbled

1  Preheat oven to 200°C/400°F.
2  Roll pastry into 28cm x 30cm (11 inch x 12 inch) rectangle; place on oiled oven tray. Fold edges of pastry over to make a 1cm (½ inch) border all the way around pastry. Prick pastry base with fork; bake 10 minutes.
3  Meanwhile, heat half the oil in medium frying pan; cook lamb, coriander and cinnamon, stirring, 5 minutes. Drain away excess oil.
4  Combine chickpeas, garlic, juice and remaining oil in medium bowl. Using fork, coarsely mash mixture; stir in preserved lemon. Spread mixture over pastry base. Top with lamb mixture; sprinkle with nuts and cheese. Bake, in oven, about 10 minutes.

prep + cook time 45 minutes  serves 4
nutritional count per serving  34.8g total fat
(14.3g saturated fat); 2274kJ (544 cal);
27.7g carbohydrate; 28.4g protein; 4.4g fibre

note  To use preserved lemon rind, remove and discard pulp; squeeze and discard juice from rind, then rinse rind well. Slice according to the recipe.

# prosciutto-wrapped pork and veal meatloaf

4 slices white bread (180g), crusts removed
½ cup (125ml) milk
300g (9½ ounces) minced (ground) pork
450g (14½ ounces) minced (ground) veal
1 small leek (200g), chopped finely
2 cloves garlic, crushed
2 teaspoons fresh thyme leaves
½ cup finely chopped fresh flat-leaf parsley
½ cup (40g) finely grated parmesan cheese
2 eggs
8 slices prosciutto (120g)
1 tablespoon dijon mustard

1  Preheat oven to 200°C/400°F.
2  Tear bread into pieces; pour milk over bread in large bowl, stand 2 minutes.
3  Add minces, leek, garlic, herbs, cheese and eggs to bowl; mix well. Roughly mould mixture into a cylinder shape.
4  Lay 6 slices of prosciutto on board, overlapping slightly; brush with mustard. Place mince mound onto prosciutto slices; using wet hands, pat mixture into loaf shape. Lay remaining 2 slices prosciutto lengthways on top of meatloaf. Wrap bottom prosciutto slices around sides of meatloaf to meet slices on top. Turn meatloaf over carefully; place on wire rack set in large shallow baking dish.
5  Cook meatloaf, uncovered, about 1 hour or until juices run clear. Cover meatloaf; stand 10 minutes before serving.

**prep + cook time** 1 hour  20 minutes  **serves** 4
**nutritional count per serving** 23.4g total fat (9.6g saturated fat); 2266kJ (542 cal); 23.4g carbohydrate; 58g protein; 2.9g fibre

# lamb and burghul burgers

½ cup (80g) burghul
½ cup (125ml) boiling water
250g (8 ounces) minced (ground) lamb
1 small brown onion (80g), chopped finely
1 small zucchini (90g), grated coarsely
¼ cup finely chopped fresh mint
1 egg
1 tablespoon olive oil
4 turkish bread rolls (660g)
½ baby cos (romaine) lettuce, torn
1 large tomato (220g), sliced thinly
1 cup (240g) hummus

1  Place burghul in small bowl, cover with the water; stand 10 minutes or until burghul softens and water is absorbed.
2  Combine burghul in medium bowl with lamb, onion, zucchini, mint and egg. Shape mixture into four patties.
3  Heat oil in large frying pan; cook patties, over medium heat, until browned both sides and cooked through.
4  Meanwhile, preheat grill (broiler).
5  Split rolls in half; toast cut sides. Sandwich lettuce, patties, tomato and hummus between roll halves.

**prep + cook time** 45 minutes  **serves** 4
**nutritional count per serving**  28.3g total fat (6.9g saturated fat); 3407kJ (815 cal); 94.2g carbohydrate; 38.3g protein; 14.7g fibre

# beef and eggplant bake with polenta crust

2 medium eggplants (600g), sliced thickly
2 tablespoons coarse cooking salt
1 tablespoon olive oil
1 medium brown onion (150g), chopped coarsely
1 medium red capsicum (bell pepper) (200g), chopped coarsely
1 clove garlic, crushed
500g (1 pound) minced (ground) beef
2 tablespoons tomato paste
½ cup (125ml) dry red wine
400g (12½ ounces) canned whole tomatoes
1 cup firmly packed fresh basil leaves
1 tablespoon fresh oregano leaves
2 cups (500ml) chicken stock
2 cups (500ml) milk
1 cup (170g) polenta
1½ cups (150g) coarsely grated mozzarella cheese

1  Place eggplant in colander, sprinkle all over with salt; stand 30 minutes. Rinse eggplant; drain on absorbent paper.
2  Meanwhile, heat oil in medium frying pan; cook onion, capsicum and garlic, stirring, until onion softens. Add mince; cook, stirring, until mince changes colour. Add paste; cook, stirring, 2 minutes. Add wine; cook, stirring, 5 minutes. Add undrained tomatoes; bring to the boil. Simmer, uncovered, stirring occasionally, about 15 minutes or until liquid is almost evaporated.
3  Chop about a quarter of the basil leaves coarsely; stir into sauce with oregano.
4  Preheat oven to 200°C/400°F.
5  Cook eggplant on heated oiled grill plate (or grill or barbecue) until just browned.
6  Meanwhile, combine stock and milk in medium saucepan; bring to the boil. Gradually add polenta, stirring constantly. Simmer, stirring constantly, about 10 minutes or until polenta thickens.
7  Arrange half the eggplant in a shallow 3-litre (12-cup) baking dish; top with half the mince mixture. Top with remaining eggplant then remaining mince mixture and remaining basil. Spread polenta over basil; sprinkle with cheese. Cook, uncovered, in oven, about 20 minutes or until top is browned lightly. Stand 10 minutes before serving with a mixed green salad.

prep + cook time 1 hour 40 minutes (+ standing)
serves 6
nutritional count per serving  19g total fat
(8.8g saturated fat); 1894kJ (453 cal);
31.9g carbohydrate; 23.4g protein; 5.3g fibre

# keema with green chilli and tomato

2 tablespoons ghee
1 medium brown onion (150g), chopped finely
5cm (2 inch) piece fresh ginger (25g), grated
2 cloves garlic, crushed
3 fresh long green chillies, chopped finely
2 teaspoons each cumin seeds, ground coriander
  and garam masala
1 teaspoon ground turmeric
800g (1½ pounds) minced (ground) lamb
400g (12½ ounces) canned diced tomatoes
2 large tomatoes (440g), chopped coarsely
⅓ cup (95g) yogurt
1 tablespoon lemon juice
1 cup (120g) frozen peas
2 tablespoons coarsely chopped fresh
  coriander (cilantro)

1  Heat ghee in large saucepan; cook onion, ginger, garlic and two-thirds of the chilli, stirring, until onion softens. Add spices; cook, stirring, until fragrant. Add mince; cook, stirring, until mince changes colour.
2  Add undrained tomatoes and fresh tomato to pan; cook, stirring occasionally, about 15 minutes or until mince is cooked through and sauce has thickened.
3  Add remaining chilli, yogurt, juice and peas; cook, uncovered, until peas are just tender. Serve curry sprinkled with coriander, and accompany with naan bread, to soak up the juices, if you like.

**prep + cook time** 1 hour  **serves** 4
**nutritional count per serving**  4.6g total fat
(2.4g saturated fat); 364kJ (87 cal);
2.2g carbohydrate; 8.8g protein; 1.2g fibre

# chilli con carne with quesadillas

1 tablespoon olive oil
300g (9½ ounces) minced (ground) beef
1 medium red onion (170g), chopped finely
2 cloves garlic, crushed
1 tablespoon worcestershire sauce
1 tablespoon Tabasco sauce
2 teaspoons each ground cumin and coriander
1 teaspoon dried oregano
400g (12½ ounces) canned crushed tomatoes
½ cup (130g) chunky tomato salsa
400g (12½ ounces) canned kidney beans,
　　rinsed, drained
400g (12½ ounces) canned chickpeas (garbanzo),
　　rinsed, drained

QUESADILLAS
¾ cup (90g) coarsely grated cheddar cheese
4 x 20cm (8 inch) flour tortillas
30g (1 ounce) butter

1   Heat half the oil in medium saucepan; cook
beef, stirring, until browned, remove from pan.
Heat remaining oil in same pan; cook onion and
garlic, stirring, until onion softens. Return beef to
pan with sauces, cumin, coriander and oregano;
cook, stirring, 2 minutes.
2   Add undrained tomatoes then stir in salsa, beans
and chickpeas; cook, uncovered, 10 minutes.
3   Meanwhile, make quesadillas. Serve chilli
with quesadillas.

quesadillas  Divide the cheese between two tortillas;
top with remaining tortillas, pressing firmly to seal.
Heat butter in medium frying pan; cook until browned
both sides. Cut each quesadilla into quarters.

prep + cook time 35 minutes  serves 4
nutritional count per serving  26.8g total fat
(11.1g saturated fat); 2562kJ (613 cal);
51.7g carbohydrate; 35.5g protein; 11.6g fibre

# meat pies

1½ cups (225g) plain (all-purpose) flour
90g (3 ounces) cold butter, chopped coarsely
1 egg
1 tablespoon iced water, approximately
2 sheets ready-rolled puff pastry
1 egg, extra

BEEF FILLING
1 tablespoon vegetable oil
1 small brown onion (80g), chopped finely
600g (1¼ pounds) minced (ground) beef
400g (12½ ounces) canned crushed tomatoes
2 tablespoons tomato paste
2 tablespoons worcestershire sauce
¾ cup (180ml) beef stock

1  Process flour and butter until crumbly. Add egg and enough of the water to make ingredients cling together. Knead pastry on lightly floured surface until smooth. Cover; refrigerate 30 minutes.
2  Meanwhile, make beef filling.
3  Oil six ⅔-cup (160ml) pie tins. Divide pastry into six portions; roll each between sheets of baking paper (parchment) until large enough to line tins. Lift pastry into tins; gently press over base and sides; trim. Refrigerate 30 minutes.
4  Cut six 11cm (4½ inch) rounds from puff pastry. Refrigerate until required.
5  Preheat oven to 200°C/400°F.
6  Place pastry cases on oven tray; line pastry with baking paper then fill with dried beans or uncooked rice. Bake 10 minutes; remove paper and beans. Bake a further 5 minutes; cool.
7  Fill pastry cases with beef filling; brush edges of pastry with extra egg. Top with puff pastry rounds; press edges to seal. Brush tops with egg. Cut steam holes in top of pies. Bake about 20 minutes or until pastry is golden. Serve pies with tomato sauce.

beef filling  Heat oil in large saucepan, add onion and beef; cook, stirring, until beef is well browned. Stir in undrained tomatoes, paste, sauce and stock; bring to the boil. Reduce heat, simmer, uncovered, about 20 minutes or until thick. Cool.

prep + cook time 1 hour 35 minutes (+ refrigeration)
makes 6
nutritional count per pie  38.7g total fat
(13.8g saturated fat); 2876kJ (688 cal);
52.4g carbohydrate; 31.2g protein; 3.5g fibre

# sang choy bow

2 teaspoons sesame oil
1 small brown onion (80g), chopped finely
2 cloves garlic, crushed
2cm (¾ inch) piece fresh ginger (10g), grated
500g (1 pound) minced (ground) pork
2 tablespoons water
100g (3 ounces) shiitake mushrooms, chopped finely
2 tablespoons each light soy sauce and
  oyster sauce
1 tablespoon lime juice
2 cups bean sprouts
4 green onions (scallions), sliced thinly
¼ cup coarsely chopped fresh coriander (cilantro)
12 large butter (boston) lettuce leaves

1   Heat oil in wok; stir-fry brown onion, garlic and
ginger until onion softens. Add pork; stir-fry until
changed in colour.
2   Add the water, mushrooms, sauces and juice;
stir-fry until mushrooms are tender. Remove from
heat. Add sprouts, green onion and coriander; toss
to combine.
3   Spoon sang choy bow into lettuce leaves to serve.

**prep + cook time** 30 minutes  **serves** 4
**nutritional count per serving**  11.5g total fat
(3.6g saturated fat); 1112kJ (266 cal);
8.9g carbohydrate; 29.3g protein; 4.1g fibre

# lamb rissoles with potato crush and rosemary gravy

500g (1 pound) minced (ground) lamb
1 large brown onion (200g), grated coarsely
1 clove garlic, crushed
½ cup (35g) fresh breadcrumbs
1 egg
1 tablespoon olive oil
500g (1 pound) baby new potatoes
30g (1 ounce) butter
1 tablespoon plain (all-purpose) flour
1 cup (250ml) beef stock
1 tablespoon fresh rosemary leaves
250g (8 ounces) cherry tomatoes

1  Combine lamb, onion, garlic, breadcrumbs
and egg in medium bowl. Shape mixture into
eight rissoles.
2  Heat oil in large frying pan; cook rissoles, in
batches, about 15 minutes or until cooked through.
Drain on absorbent paper; cover with foil to keep
warm. Reserve pan with rissole drippings.
3  Meanwhile, boil, steam or microwave potatoes
until tender; drain. Crush potatoes in medium bowl
with potato masher; stir in butter.
4  Cook flour in rissole pan, stirring, until mixture
browns and bubbles. Gradually stir in stock; stir
until gravy boils and thickens. Strain gravy; stir
in rosemary.
5  Meanwhile, cook tomatoes, stirring, in heated
small frying pan about 2 minutes or until split and
just softened.
6  Serve rissoles with potatoes and tomatoes;
drizzle with gravy.

prep + cook time 55 minutes  serves 4
nutritional count per serving  23.7g total fat
(10.2g saturated fat); 1898kJ (454 cal);
26.4g carbohydrate; 33.7g protein; 3.9 fibre

# chicken, tomato and fetta patties with spinach salad

750g (1½ pounds) minced (ground) chicken
⅓ cup (50g) drained semi-dried tomatoes in oil,
  chopped coarsely
1 egg
½ cup (35g) stale breadcrumbs
200g (6½ ounces) fetta cheese, crumbled
1 small white onion (80g), sliced thinly
100g (3 ounces) baby spinach leaves
1 tablespoon olive oil
1 tablespoon balsamic vinegar

**1** Combine chicken, tomato, egg, breadcrumbs
and half the cheese in large bowl; shape mixture
into 12 patties.
**2** Cook patties in heated oiled large frying pan, in
batches, until cooked through. Remove from pan.
Drain on absorbent paper.
**3** Meanwhile, combine onion, spinach, oil, vinegar
and remaining cheese in medium bowl. Serve
patties with spinach salad.

**prep + cook time** 30 minutes  **serves** 4
**nutritional count per serving**  33.7g total fat
(13.3g saturated fat); 2320kJ (555 cal);
11.8g carbohydrate; 50.1g protein; 3.2g fibre

# shepherd's pie

30g (1 ounce) butter
1 medium brown onion (150g), chopped finely
1 medium carrot (120g), chopped finely
½ teaspoon dried mixed herbs
4 cups (750g) finely chopped cooked lamb
¼ cup (70g) tomato paste
¼ cup (60ml) tomato sauce
2 tablespoons worcestershire sauce
2 cups (500ml) beef stock
2 tablespoons plain (all-purpose) flour
⅓ cup (80ml) water

POTATO TOPPING
5 medium potatoes (1kg), chopped coarsely
60g (2 ounces) butter
¼ cup (60ml) milk

1   Preheat oven to 200°C/400°F. Oil shallow
2.5-litre (10-cup) ovenproof dish.
2   Make potato topping.
3   Meanwhile, heat butter in large saucepan; cook
onion and carrot, stirring, until tender. Add mixed
herbs and lamb; cook, stirring, 2 minutes. Stir in
paste, sauces and stock, then blended flour and
water; stir over heat until mixture boils and thickens.
Pour mixture into dish.
4   Drop heaped tablespoons of potato topping
onto lamb mixture. Bake in oven about 20 minutes
or until browned and heated through.

potato topping   Boil, steam or microwave potato
until tender; drain. Mash with butter and milk until
mixture is smooth.

prep + cook time 1 hour  serves 4
nutritional count per serving  36.2g total fat
(20.2g saturated fat); 2976kJ (712 cal);
44.7g carbohydrate; 48.8g protein; 6g fibre

# lamb kofta with chilli tomato and yogurt sauce

1kg (2 pounds) minced (ground) lamb
1 large brown onion (200g), chopped finely
1 clove garlic, crushed
1 tablespoon ground cumin
2 teaspoons each ground turmeric and allspice
1 tablespoon finely chopped fresh mint
2 tablespoons finely chopped fresh flat-leaf parsley
1 egg, beaten lightly
6 pocket pitta breads (510g), quartered

YOGURT SAUCE
¾ cup (200g) low-fat yogurt
1 clove garlic, crushed
1 tablespoon finely chopped fresh flat-leaf parsley

CHILLI TOMATO SAUCE
¼ cup (60ml) tomato sauce (ketchup)
¼ cup (60ml) chilli sauce

1  Make yogurt sauce; make chilli tomato sauce.
2  Combine lamb, onion, garlic, spices, herbs and egg in large bowl. Divide mixture into 18 even-sized pieces; mould around skewers to form sausage shapes.
3  Cook kofta, in batches, on heated oiled grill plate (or grill or barbecue) until cooked through.
4  Serve kofta with pitta, yogurt sauce and chilli tomato sauce.

yogurt sauce  Combine ingredients in small bowl.

chilli tomato sauce  Combine sauces in small bowl.

prep + cook time 30 minutes  serves 6
nutritional count per serving  14.1g total fat (5.7g saturated fat); 1931kJ (462 cal); 38.2g carbohydrate; 43.2g protein; 3.1g fibre

note  Soak 18 bamboo skewers in water for at least 30 minutes to prevent scorching during cooking, or cover the ends with foil.
Serve with tabbouleh or a greek salad.

# simple mince stir-fries

## chilli chicken with broccoli and cashews

Heat 2 teaspoons peanut oil in wok; stir-fry 600g (1¼ pounds) minced (ground) chicken until cooked. Remove from wok. Heat 2 teaspoons peanut oil in wok; stir-fry 1 crushed garlic clove and 1 small thinly sliced brown onion, until onion softens. Add 300g (9½ ounces) broccoli florets; stir-fry until almost tender. Return chicken to wok with 2 tablespoons fish sauce, 1 tablespoon hot chilli sauce, 8 thinly sliced green onions (scallions), 1¼ cups bean sprouts, ⅓ cup roasted unsalted cashews and 4 thinly sliced kaffir lime leaves; stir-fry just until hot. Remove from heat; sprinkle with 1 thinly sliced fresh long red chilli.

**prep + cook time** 30 minutes  **serves** 4
**nutritional count per serving**  23.4g total fat (5.6g saturated fat); 1643kJ (393 cal); 6.3g carbohydrate; 36.9g protein; 5.8g fibre

## beef in black bean sauce with rice noodles and greens

Place 250g (8 ounces) dried rice stick noodles in large heatproof bowl, cover with boiling water; stand until just tender, drain. Meanwhile, heat 1 tablespoon peanut oil in wok; stir-fry 600g (1¼ pounds) minced (ground) beef, 1 medium thinly sliced brown onion and 2 thinly sliced fresh long red chillies until beef is cooked through. Add 350g (11 ounces) coarsely chopped wombok (napa cabbage) and 150g (4½ ounces) sugar snap peas; stir-fry until wombok is tender. Add noodles and ¼ cup each black bean sauce, kecap manis and beef stock, 1 tablespoon rice vinegar and 4 thinly sliced green onions (scallions); stir-fry until hot.

**prep + cook time** 30 minutes  **serves** 4
**nutritional count per serving**  16.4g total fat (6.4g saturated fat); 1559kJ (373 cal); 19.2g carbohydrate; 35.2g protein; 3.3g fibre

## japanese stir-fried pork with rice noodles

Place 450g (14½ ounces) fresh wide rice noodles in large heatproof bowl, cover with boiling water; separate with fork, drain. Heat 1 tablespoon vegetable oil in wok; stir-fry 500g (1 pound) minced (ground) pork until browned. Add 2 crushed garlic cloves, 1 tablespoon sambal oelek, 4 thinly sliced green onions (scallions) and 1 tablespoon kecap manis; stir-fry 1 minute. Add noodles, ¼ cup kecap manis and 2 baby buk choy, leaves separated, to wok; stir-fry until hot. Sprinkle with 1 cup loosely packed fresh coriander (cilantro) leaves.

**prep + cook time** 25 minutes  **serves** 4
**nutritional count per serving**  14.5g total fat
(3.8g saturated fat); 1927kJ (461 cal);
49g carbohydrate; 31.1g protein; 2.8g fibre

## beef chow mein

Heat 1 tablespoon vegetable oil in wok; stir-fry 500g (1 pound) minced (ground) beef, 1 finely chopped medium brown onion and 2 crushed garlic cloves until beef is browned. Add 1 tablespoon curry powder; stir-fry 1 minute or until fragrant. Add 1 finely chopped large carrot, 2 trimmed, thinly sliced, celery stalks and 150g (4½ ounces) thinly sliced button mushrooms; stir-fry until vegetables soften. Add 1 cup chicken stock, ⅓ cup oyster sauce, 2 tablespoons dark soy sauce, 440g (14 ounces) thin fresh egg noodles; stir-fry 2 minutes. Add ½ cup frozen peas and ½ small coarsely shredded wombok (napa cabbage); stir-fry until wombok just wilts.

**prep + cook time** 50 minutes  **serves** 4
**nutritional count per serving**  15.7g total fat
(4.6g saturated fat); 2571kJ (615 cal);
70.6g carbohydrate; 42.3g protein; 8.4g fibre

# sausages

## pork sausages with grilled polenta and spicy tomato sauce

1 litre (4 cups) water
1 cup (170g) polenta
1 cup (120g) coarsely grated cheddar cheese
2 teaspoons olive oil
1 medium red onion (170g), sliced thinly
1 clove garlic, crushed
1 fresh small red thai chilli (serrano), chopped finely
4 medium tomatoes (600g), chopped coarsely
8 thick pork sausages (960g)

1 Bring the water to the boil in medium saucepan; gradually stir in polenta. Simmer, stirring, until polenta thickens. Stir in cheese. Spread polenta into oiled deep 19cm (7½ inch) square cake pan, cover; refrigerate 1 hour or until polenta firms.
2 Heat oil in medium saucepan; cook onion, garlic and chilli, stirring, until onion softens. Add tomato; simmer, covered, until tomato softens.
3 Cut polenta into quarters. Cook polenta and sausages, in batches, on heated oiled grill plate (or grill or barbecue) until polenta is browned both sides and sausages are cooked through.
4 Serve sausages on polenta squares, topped with spicy tomato sauce. Sprinkle with fresh thyme leaves or parsley to serve, if you like.

prep + cook time 35 minutes (+ refrigeration)
serves 4
nutritional count per serving 65.6g total fat (28.3g saturated fat); 3908kJ (935 cal); 42.2g carbohydrate; 42g protein; 6.8g fibre

# curried sausages

800g (1½ pounds) thick beef sausages
30g (1 ounce) butter
1 medium brown onion (150g), chopped coarsely
1 tablespoon curry powder
2 teaspoons plain (all-purpose) flour
2 large carrots (360g), chopped coarsely
2 celery stalks (300g), trimmed, chopped coarsely
500g (1 pound) baby new potatoes, halved
2 cups (500ml) beef stock
1 cup loosely packed fresh flat-leaf parsley leaves

**1** Cook sausages, in batches, in heated deep large frying pan until cooked through. Remove from pan. Cut each sausage into thirds.
**2** Melt butter in same cleaned pan; cook onion, stirring, until soft. Add curry powder and flour; cook, stirring, 2 minutes.
**3** Add vegetables and stock to pan; bring to the boil. Simmer, covered, about 15 minutes or until vegetables are tender. Add sausages; simmer, uncovered, until sauce thickens slightly. Stir in parsley.

**prep + cook time** 1 hour 5 minutes  **serves** 4
**nutritional count per serving** 55.8g total fat (27.3g saturated fat); 3177kJ (760 cal); 29.8g carbohydrate; 30.1g protein; 12.8g fibre

# baked risotto with
# spicy sausage and cherry tomatoes

5 thin spicy italian-style sausages (400g)
3½ cups (875ml) chicken stock
2 teaspoons olive oil
1 large brown onion (200g), chopped finely
1 clove garlic, crushed
1½ cups (300g) arborio rice
250g (8 ounces) cherry tomatoes
2 tablespoons fresh marjoram leaves

1  Preheat oven to 180°C/350°F.
2  Cook sausages in heated large frying pan until cooked through. Drain on absorbent paper, then slice thickly.
3  Meanwhile, bring stock to the boil in medium saucepan. Reduce heat; simmer, covered.
4  Heat oil in same frying pan; cook onion and garlic, stirring, until onion softens. Add rice; stir to coat in onion mixture. Stir in stock and sausages.
5  Place risotto mixture in large shallow ovenproof dish; cover with foil. Bake in oven 15 minutes, stirring halfway through cooking time. Uncover; bake a further 15 minutes. Add tomatoes; bake about 15 minutes or until tomatoes soften and rice is tender. Remove from oven; sprinkle with marjoram.

**prep + cook time** 1 hour 15 minutes  **serves** 4
**nutritional count per serving**  29.1g total fat
(13g saturated fat); 2587kJ (619 cal);
67.1g carbohydrate; 20.1g protein; 5g fibre

# warm lentil and sausage salad

1 cup (200g) brown lentils
3 medium tomatoes (450g), quartered
1 tablespoon olive oil
1 medium brown onion (150g), chopped finely
1 teaspoon ground cumin
8 thick chicken sausages (960g)
½ cup coarsely chopped fresh flat-leaf parsley

WHITE WINE VINAIGRETTE
⅓ cup (80ml) white wine vinegar
¼ cup (60ml) olive oil
1 clove garlic, crushed

1  Make white wine vinaigrette.
2  Preheat oven to 220°C/425°F.
3  Cook lentils, uncovered, in large saucepan of boiling water until just tender; drain. Place lentils in large bowl with half the vinaigrette; toss gently to combine.
4  Place tomato on oven tray; drizzle with half the oil. Roast, uncovered, in oven, about 10 minutes or until tender.
5  Meanwhile, heat remaining oil in large frying pan; cook onion and cumin, stirring, until onion softens. Transfer onion mixture to bowl with lentils.
6  Cook sausages in same pan until cooked through. Drain on absorbent paper, then slice thickly.
7  Add remaining vinaigrette, sausage, tomato and parsley to bowl with lentil mixture; toss gently.

white wine vinaigrette  Combine ingredients in screw-top jar; shake well.

prep + cook time 1 hour  serves 4
nutritional count per serving  73.6g total fat (21g saturated fat); 4034kJ (965 cal); 28.3g carbohydrate; 41.8g protein: 16.4g fibre

# mexican beans with sausages

1 cup (200g) dried kidney beans
800g (1½ pounds) thick beef sausages
1 tablespoon olive oil
1 large white onion (200g), chopped coarsely
3 cloves garlic, crushed
1 large red capsicum (bell pepper) (350g),
  chopped coarsely
½ teaspoon ground cumin
2 teaspoons sweet smoked paprika
1 teaspoon dried chilli flakes
800g (1½ pounds) canned crushed tomatoes
2 tablespoons coarsely chopped fresh oregano

1  Place beans in medium bowl, cover with cold water; stand overnight, drain. Rinse under cold water; drain.
2  Place beans in medium saucepan of boiling water; return to the boil. Simmer, uncovered, about 30 minutes or until beans are almost tender. Drain.
3  Cook sausages, in batches, in heated oiled large deep saucepan until browned. Remove from pan. Drain on absorbent paper, then slice thickly.
4  Heat oil in same pan; cook onion, garlic and capsicum, stirring, until onion softens. Add cumin, paprika and chilli; cook, stirring, about 2 minutes or until fragrant. Add beans and undrained tomatoes; bring to the boil. Simmer, covered, about 1 hour or until beans are tender.
5  Return sausages to pan; simmer, covered, about 10 minutes or until sausages are heated through. Remove from heat; stir in oregano.

**prep + cook time** 2 hours 35 minutes (+ standing)
**serves** 4
**nutritional count per serving** 56.9g total fat (25.2g saturated fat); 3323 kJ (795 cal); 33.5g carbohydrate; 38.1g protein; 20.2g fibre

**note**  This is one of those dishes that tastes even better the next day when the flavours have had time to amalgamate.
**Serve with** tortillas.

# italian sausage and three-cheese lasagne

500g (1 pound) italian sausages
250g (8 ounces) frozen chopped spinach,
 thawed, drained
250g (8 ounces) ricotta cheese
¼ teaspoon ground nutmeg
½ cup (40g) finely grated parmesan cheese
1 egg
6 sheets fresh lasagne
250g (8 ounces) mozzarella cheese, sliced thinly

TOMATO SAUCE
1 tablespoon olive oil
1 medium onion (150g), chopped finely
1 medium carrot (120g), chopped finely
1 celery stalk (150g), trimmed, chopped finely
5 long parsley stalks, crushed
2 cloves garlic, crushed
½ cup (125ml) dry red wine
¼ cup (70g) tomato paste
700g (1½ pounds) bottled tomato pasta sauce

CHEESE SAUCE
60g (2 ounces) butter
⅓ cup (50g) plain (all-purpose) flour
2 cups (500ml) milk
1½ cups (120g) finely grated parmesan cheese

1  Make tomato sauce. Make cheese sauce.
2  Preheat oven to 200°C/400°F.
3  Cook sausages in oiled large frying pan until browned all over; drain, then slice thinly.
4  Combine spinach, ricotta, nutmeg, parmesan and egg in medium bowl.
5  Spread ½ cup of the cheese sauce over base of 20cm x 30cm (8 inch x 12 inch) ovenproof dish. Top with two pasta sheets (cut to fit dish) then spread with half the spinach mixture. Sprinkle with half the sausage; cover with 1 cup of the tomato sauce, then half the remaining cheese sauce.
6  Top mixture with two more pasta sheets. Spread remaining spinach mixture over pasta; sprinkle with remaining sausage. Spread with 1 cup tomato sauce, then remaining cheese sauce.
7  Top with remaining pasta, then half the remaining tomato sauce. Top with mozzarella, then spread with remaining tomato sauce.
8  Bake lasagne, covered, 30 minutes. Uncover, bake about 10 minutes or until browned lightly. Stand 10 minutes before serving.

tomato sauce Heat oil in large saucepan, add onion, carrot, celery and parsley; cook, stirring occasionally, until vegetables soften. Add garlic; cook, stirring, 1 minute. Add wine; cook, stirring, until almost evaporated. Discard parsley stalks. Add paste; cook, stirring, 3 minutes. Add sauce; simmer, uncovered, about 15 minutes.

cheese sauce Melt butter in medium saucepan, add flour; cook, stirring, until mixture thickens and bubbles. Gradually add milk; stir until mixture boils and thickens. Reduce heat; cook, stirring, 1 minute, remove from heat. Add cheese; stir until melted.

prep + cook time 2 hours 40 minutes serves 8
nutritional count per serving 46.8g total fat (23.1g saturated fat); 3227kJ (772 cal); 44g carbohydrate; 39.3g protein; 5.4g fibre

# italian braised sausages with beans

8 thick beef sausages (1.2kg)
2 x 400g (12½ ounces) canned diced tomatoes
⅓ cup (80ml) water
200g (6½ ounces) drained marinated antipasto vegetables
400g (12½ ounces) canned cannellini beans, rinsed, drained
½ cup loosely packed fresh baby basil leaves

1  Cook sausages in heated oiled large saucepan until browned. Remove from pan; cut sausages in half lengthways.
2  Add undrained tomatoes and the water to same pan; bring to the boil. Return sausages to pan with antipasto vegetables; simmer, covered, 15 minutes.
3  Add beans to pan; simmer, uncovered, about 10 minutes or until thickened slightly.
4  Remove from heat, stir in half the basil; serve topped with remaining basil.

**prep + cook time** 35 minutes  **serves** 4
**nutritional count per serving**  78.1g total fat (36.9g saturated fat); 4113kJ (983 cal); 23g carbohydrate; 41.9g protein; 16g fibre

**note**  We used semi-dried tomatoes, marinated artichokes, grilled eggplant and red capsicum for the antipasto mix; however, any combination of vegetables can be used.

# warm split pea and sausage salad

1½ cups (300g) yellow split peas
2 rindless bacon slices (130g), chopped coarsely
6 thin sausages (480g), chopped coarsely
1 medium carrot (120g), chopped coarsely
1 celery stalk (150g), trimmed, chopped coarsely
1 medium brown onion (150g), chopped coarsely
2 cloves garlic, sliced thinly
250g (8 ounces) grape tomatoes, halved
400g (12½ ounces) canned white beans,
  rinsed, drained
2 teaspoons finely grated orange rind
⅓ cup (80ml) orange juice

1  Place peas in medium bowl, cover with cold water; stand overnight, drain. Rinse under cold water; drain.
2  Place peas in medium saucepan, cover with boiling water. Simmer, covered, about 10 minutes or until peas are tender; rinse under cold water, drain.
3  Meanwhile, cook bacon and sausage in large heated saucepan, in batches, until sausage is cooked. Remove from pan.
4  Add carrot, celery, onion and garlic to pan; cook, stirring, until carrot softens slightly. Add tomatoes; cook, stirring, 2 minutes. Add beans, peas, bacon and sausage; stir to combine. Remove from heat; stir in rind and juice.

prep + cook time 40 minutes (+ standing)  serves 4
nutritional count per serving  33.9g total fat
(15.1g saturated fat); 2985kJ (714 cal);
51.2g carbohydrate; 43g protein; 16.8g fibre

note  We used thin lamb merguez sausages.

31

# posh sausage sambos

8 thick lamb, rosemary and garlic sausages (680g)
1 loaf turkish bread (430g)
½ cup (140g) tomato relish
2 cups firmly packed trimmed watercress

CARAMELISED ONION
2 tablespoons olive oil
4 medium brown onions (600g), sliced thinly
1 tablespoon light brown sugar
¼ cup (60ml) red wine vinegar

1  Make caramelised onion.
2  Cook sausages in heated oiled large frying pan until cooked through. Drain on absorbent paper, then halve sausages lengthways.
3  Meanwhile, split bread lengthways; spread top with relish, spread base with caramelised onion. Sandwich sausage halves and watercress between bread slices; press top on firmly.

caramelised onion  Heat oil in large frying pan; cook onion, stirring, over low heat, about 10 minutes or until soft. Add sugar and vinegar; cook, stirring, about 10 minutes or until onion is caramelised. Cool.

prep + cook time 45 minutes (+ cooling)  serves 8
nutritional count per serving  21.5g total fat (7.4g saturated fat); 1927kJ (461 cal); 38.2g carbohydrate; 27.1g protein; 3.5g fibre

# spicy sausage pasta bake

375g (12 ounces) tortiglioni pasta
6 spicy lamb sausages (900g)
1 medium brown onion (150g), chopped coarsely
1 small eggplant (230g), chopped coarsely
2 medium red capsicums (bell peppers) (400g),
  chopped coarsely
3 small green zucchini (270g), chopped coarsely
700g (1½ pounds) bottled tomato pasta sauce
½ cup coarsely chopped fresh basil
2 cups (200g) grated pizza cheese

1  Preheat oven to 180°C/350°F.
2  Cook pasta in large saucepan of boiling water
until just tender; drain.
3  Meanwhile, cook sausages in oiled large frying
pan until just cooked through. Drain on absorbent
paper, then cut into 2.5cm (1 inch) slices.
4  Cook onion, eggplant, capsicum and zucchini,
stirring, in same pan until just tender. Add sausage,
sauce and basil; stir to combine.
5  Combine pasta and sausage mixture in deep
3-litre (12-cup) casserole dish; sprinkle with cheese.
Bake about 20 minutes or until browned lightly.

**prep + cook time** 50 minutes  **serves** 6
**nutritional count per serving**  36.3g total fat
(16.5g saturated fat); 3453kJ (826 cal);
67.7g carbohydrate; 57.6g protein; 7.5g fibre

**note** Tortiglioni is a straight tubular pasta with
grooves on the exterior; it works well when baked
with a chunky sauce. You can substitute it with
rigatoni, if you like.

# fast sausages

## salami and rocket pizza

Preheat oven to 200°C/400°F. Place 2 x 25cm (10 inch) pizza bases on oven trays. Spread ⅔ cup bottled tomato pasta sauce evenly over bases; top with 250g (8 ounces) thinly sliced mozzarella cheese and 125g (4 ounces) thinly sliced salami. Bake about 15 minutes or until cheese melts and bases are crisp. Just before serving, top pizzas with 50g (1¾ ounces) baby rocket leaves (arugula).

**prep + cook time** 25 minutes  **serves** 4
**nutritional count per serving**  30.3g total fat
(13.3g saturated fat); 2855kJ (683 cal);
65.9g carbohydrate; 34.3g protein; 5.2g fibre

## grilled pork sausages with fruit relish

Heat 1 tablespoon oil in medium saucepan; cook 1 small finely chopped red onion and 1 crushed garlic clove, stirring, until onion softens. Add 2 finely chopped medium pears, ¼ cup finely chopped dried apricots, ¼ cup sultanas, 2 tablespoons cider vinegar, 2 tablespoons light brown sugar and ½ teaspoon ground allspice; cook, uncovered, stirring occasionally, about 10 minutes or until mixture is thick and pulpy. Meanwhile, cook 12 thick pork sausages on heated oiled grill plate (or grill or barbecue) until cooked through. Serve sausages with fruit relish.

**prep + cook time** 30 minutes  **serves** 6
**nutritional count per serving**  58.7g total fat
(22.9g saturated fat); 3252kJ (778 cal);
29.9g carbohydrate; 31g protein; 6.2g fibre

## sausages with the lot

Cook 12 beef chipolatas in heated oiled medium frying pan until cooked through; remove from pan. Cook 1 thickly sliced large brown onion in same heated pan until onion softens. Add 4 coarsely chopped medium tomatoes and ½ teaspoon dried chilli flakes; cook, stirring occasionally, about 10 minutes or until tomato softens; season. Meanwhile, preheat grill (broiler). Return sausages to pan. Carefully crack 4 eggs into pan; cook under grill about 5 minutes or until eggs are just set. Serve sprinkled with ⅓ cup coarsely chopped fresh flat-leaf parsley.

**prep + cook time** 30 minutes  **serves** 4
**nutritional count per serving**  28.3g total fat (12.6g saturated fat); 1530kJ (366 cal); 6.9g carbohydrate; 19.2g protein; 4.9g fibre

## sausages with tomato relish

Heat 1 tablespoon olive oil in small saucepan; cook 1 crushed garlic clove and 1 finely chopped medium brown onion, stirring, until browned lightly. Add 2 large, coarsely chopped tomatoes, 1 tablespoon balsamic vinegar and 1 teaspoon light brown sugar; simmer, uncovered, stirring occasionally, about 20 minutes or until mixture is reduced by half. Just before serving, add 1 tablespoon torn fresh basil leaves. Meanwhile, cook 8 thin pork sausages on heated oiled grill plate (or grill or barbecue) until cooked through. Serve sausages with warm tomato relish.

**prep + cook time** 25 minutes  **serves** 4
**nutritional count per serving**  30.5g total fat (11.1g saturated fat); 1576kJ (377 cal); 9g carbohydrate; 15.8g protein; 3.6g fibre

# vegetables

## vegetarian tarts

1kg (2 pounds) potatoes, chopped coarsely
½ cup (125ml) hot vegetable stock
30g (1 ounce) butter
2 cloves garlic, crushed
200g (6½ ounces) button mushrooms, sliced thickly
2 tablespoons finely shredded fresh basil
2 green onions (scallions), chopped finely
⅔ cup (80g) coarsely grated cheddar cheese
3 sheets fillo pastry
30g (1 ounce) butter, melted

1  Boil, steam or microwave potato until tender; drain. Mash potato with stock until smooth.
2  Meanwhile, melt butter in small frying pan; cook garlic and mushrooms, stirring, until mushrooms soften. Stir mushroom mixture, basil, onion and half the cheese into potato mixture.
3  Preheat oven to 200°C/400°F. Oil four 1-cup (250ml) metal pie dishes. Place a 2.5cm x 30cm (1 inch x 12 inch) strip of baking paper (parchment) over base of each dish, extending 5cm (2 inches) over sides of dishes.
4  Stack pastry sheets; cut stack in half crossways. Brush between layers with melted butter, then cut stack into four squares. Line pie dishes with squares. Spoon potato mixture into dishes; sprinkle with remaining cheese.
5  Place dishes on oven tray; bake tarts in oven about 15 minutes or until pastry is browned lightly. Use baking paper strips to lift tarts out of dishes.

prep + cook time 45 minutes  serves 4
nutritional count per serving  19.9g total fat (12.5g saturated fat); 1697kJ (406 cal); 39.3g carbohydrate; 14.5g protein; 5.9g fibre

# capsicums stuffed with pilaf

2 teaspoons olive oil
1 medium red onion (170g), chopped finely
1 tablespoon slivered almonds
⅔ cup (130g) white long-grain rice
1 cup (250ml) water
2 tablespoons finely chopped dried apricots
¼ cup (35g) sun-dried tomatoes, chopped finely
¼ cup finely chopped fresh flat-leaf parsley
4 medium red capsicums (bell peppers) (800g)
cooking-oil spray

ROASTED TOMATO SALAD
2 medium tomatoes (300g), cut into thick wedges
1 tablespoon cider vinegar
½ teaspoon cracked black pepper
1 teaspoon white sugar
1 cup firmly packed fresh flat-leaf parsley leaves
½ cup firmly packed fresh mint leaves

1  Preheat oven to 200°C/400°F.
2  To make pilaf, heat oil in medium saucepan; cook onion and nuts, stirring, until onion softens. Add rice; cook, stirring, 1 minute. Add the water; bring to the boil. Simmer, covered, until liquid is absorbed and rice is just tender. Stir in apricot, tomato and parsley.
3  Cut tops off capsicums; discard tops. Discard seeds and membranes, leaving capsicum intact. Divide pilaf among capsicums; place on oven tray, spray with oil. Roast, uncovered, 10 minutes. Cover loosely with foil; cook a further 20 minutes or until capsicums are just soft.
4  Meanwhile, make roasted tomato salad.
5  Serve capsicums with roasted tomato salad.

roasted tomato salad  Combine tomato with vinegar, pepper and sugar in medium bowl. Drain; reserve liquid. Place tomato on oven tray; roast, uncovered, alongside capsicums about 10 minutes or until tomato just softens. Place tomato and reserved liquid in medium bowl with herbs; toss gently.

prep + cook time 1 hour 15 minutes  serves 4
nutritional count per serving  5.7g total fat
(0.6g saturated fat); 1087kJ (260 cal);
43.4g carbohydrate; 8.2g protein; 7.3g fibre

# corn, mushroom, capsicum and potato pudding

4 medium potatoes (800g), chopped coarsely
¼ cup (60ml) milk
30g (1 ounce) butter
3 trimmed corn cobs (750g)
2 teaspoons olive oil
2 cloves garlic, crushed
1 fresh long red chilli, chopped finely
1 medium brown onion (150g), chopped coarsely
1 medium red capsicum (bell pepper) (200g),
  chopped coarsely
150g (4½ ounces) button mushrooms,
  chopped coarsely
¾ cup (90g) low-fat cheddar cheese,
  grated coarsely

1  Preheat oven to 200°C/400°F.
2  Boil, steam or microwave potato until tender;
drain. Mash potato in large bowl with milk and
butter until smooth.
3  Meanwhile, using sharp knife, cut corn kernels
from cobs. Heat oil in medium frying pan; cook
garlic, chilli and onion, stirring, until onion softens.
Add corn, capsicum and mushrooms; cook, stirring,
until corn is tender. Stir in ½ cup of the cheese.
4  Spoon corn mixture into four 1¼-cup (310ml)
ovenproof dishes; top with mashed potato and
remaining cheese. Place on oven tray; cook,
uncovered, about 25 minutes or until cheese is
browned lightly and pudding is heated through.

**prep + cook time** 50 minutes  **serves** 4
**nutritional count per serving**  14.8g total fat
(7.3g saturated fat); 1827kJ (437 cal);
49.5g carbohydrate; 20.8g protein; 11.1g fibre

# roasted vegetable lasagne

2 medium eggplants (600g), sliced thinly
2 tablespoons coarse cooking salt
3 medium red capsicums (bell peppers) (600g)
2 medium zucchini (240g), sliced thinly
1 large kumara (orange sweet potato) (500g),
  sliced thinly
cooking-oil spray
700g (1½ pounds) bottled tomato pasta sauce
4 fresh lasagne sheets, cut to fit dish
150g (4½ ounces) firm ricotta cheese, crumbled
1 tablespoon finely grated parmesan cheese

WHITE SAUCE
30g (1 ounce) butter
¼ cup (35g) plain (all-purpose) flour
1½ cups (375ml) skim milk
2 tablespoons coarsely grated parmesan cheese

1  Preheat oven to 240°C/475°F.
2  Place eggplant in colander, sprinkle with salt;
stand 20 minutes. Rinse eggplant under cold water;
pat dry with absorbent paper.
3  Quarter capsicums; discard seeds and
membranes. Roast, uncovered, skin-side up, in
oven, about 5 minutes or until skin blisters and
blackens. Cover capsicum in plastic or paper for
5 minutes, then peel away skin.
4  Reduce oven temperature to 200°C/400°F.
5  Place eggplant, zucchini and kumara in single
layer on oven trays; spray with oil. Roast, uncovered,
about 15 minutes or until tender.
6  Meanwhile, make white sauce.
7  Oil deep rectangular 2.5-litre (10-cup) ovenproof
dish. Spread 1 cup pasta sauce over base of dish;
top with half the eggplant and half the capsicum.
Layer with lasagne sheet; top with ½ cup of the pasta
sauce then ricotta, kumara and zucchini. Layer with
another lasagne sheet; top with remaining pasta
sauce, remaining eggplant and remaining capsicum.
Layer remaining lasagne sheet over vegetables; top
with white sauce, sprinkle with parmesan. Bake,
uncovered, about 45 minutes or until browned.
Stand 5 minutes before serving, with a rocket
(arugula) salad.

white sauce  Melt butter in small saucepan, add
flour; cook, stirring, until mixture thickens and
bubbles. Remove from heat, gradually stir in milk.
Return to heat; cook, stirring, until sauce boils and
thickens. Remove from heat; stir in cheese.

prep + cook time 1 hour 40 minutes (+ standing)
serves 6
nutritional count per serving  11.8g total fat
(6.4g saturated fat); 1492kJ (357 cal);
44.2g carbohydrate; 14.2g protein; 8.1g fibre

# baked mushrooms with tomato and basil

8 flat mushrooms (640g)
100g (3 ounces) enoki mushrooms,
  chopped coarsely
3 green onions (scallions), chopped finely
125g (4 ounces) grape tomatoes, halved
125g (4 ounces) cream cheese, softened
½ cup coarsely chopped fresh basil
1 cup (70g) stale breadcrumbs
2 cups (500g) bottled tomato pasta sauce
⅓ cup (25g) finely grated parmesan

1  Preheat oven to 180°C/325°F.
2  Remove stems from flat mushrooms; chop stems finely. Cook stems in heated oiled medium frying pan, stirring, until tender. Stir in enoki, onion and tomato. Cool 10 minutes.
3  Combine mushroom mixture in medium bowl with cream cheese, basil and breadcrumbs; divide mixture among mushroom caps.
4  Place pasta sauce in medium baking dish; top with mushroom caps, sprinkle mushrooms with parmesan. Bake, uncovered, about 20 minutes or until mushroom caps are tender.

prep + cook time 45 minutes  serves 4
nutritional count per serving  14.5g total fat (8.2g saturated fat); 1275kJ (305 cal); 27.9g carbohydrate; 16.2g protein; 8.4g fibre

Serve with a fresh green salad dressed in a balsamic vinaigrette.

# roasted root vegetable ratatouille

800g (1½ pounds) celeriac (celery root), trimmed,
  chopped coarsely
2 large carrots (360g), chopped coarsely
2 medium parsnips (500g), chopped coarsely
2 medium kumara (orange sweet potato) (800g),
  chopped coarsely
⅓ cup (80ml) olive oil
1 large brown onion (200g), chopped finely
3 cloves garlic, crushed
¼ cup loosely packed fresh oregano leaves
1 tablespoon tomato paste
800g (1½ pounds) canned crushed tomatoes
½ cup (125ml) dry red wine
1 cup (250ml) water
½ cup (40g) coarsely grated parmesan cheese
2½ cups (250g) coarsely grated mozzarella cheese
1 cup (70g) fresh breadcrumbs
2 teaspoons finely grated lemon rind
½ cup coarsely chopped fresh flat-leaf parsley
2 tablespoons coarsely chopped fresh oregano

1  Preheat oven to 220°C/425°F.
2  Combine celeriac, carrot, parsnip, kumara
and half the oil in deep large baking dish. Roast
vegetables, uncovered, about 50 minutes or until
vegetables are tender and browned lightly, stirring
halfway through cooking time.
3  Meanwhile, heat remaining oil in large saucepan;
cook onion, garlic and oregano leaves, stirring,
until onion softens. Add paste; cook, stirring,
1 minute. Add undrained tomatoes, wine and the
water; bring to the boil. Boil, uncovered, 10 minutes.
4  Add tomato mixture to vegetables in dish; toss
gently to combine. Sprinkle with combined cheeses,
breadcrumbs, rind, parsley and chopped oregano.
Cook, uncovered, about 20 minutes or until top
browns lightly.

**prep + cook time** 2 hours 10 minutes  **serves** 6
**nutritional count per serving**  24.7g total fat
(9.1g saturated fat); 2090 kJ (500 calories);
43.9g carbohydrate; 22.1g protein; 12.7g fibre

**Serve with** a green leafy salad.

43

# eggplant parmigiana

2 large eggplants (1kg)
vegetable oil, for shallow-frying
½ cup (75g) plain (all-purpose) flour
4 eggs, beaten lightly
2 cups (200g) packaged breadcrumbs
700g (1½ pounds) bottled tomato pasta sauce
1 cup (100g) coarsely grated mozzarella cheese
¼ cup (20g) finely grated parmesan cheese
⅓ cup loosely packed fresh oregano leaves

1  Using vegetable peeler, peel random strips of skin from eggplants; discard skins. Slice eggplants thinly.
2  Heat oil in large frying pan.
3  Coat eggplant in flour; shake off excess. Dip in egg, then in breadcrumbs. Shallow-fry eggplant, in batches, until browned lightly. Remove from pan. Drain on absorbent paper.
4  Preheat oven to 200°C/400°F.
5  Spread about one-third of the pasta sauce over base of oiled 2.5-litre (10-cup) ovenproof dish. Top with about one-third of the eggplant, one-third of the cheeses and one-third of the oregano. Repeat layering with eggplant, cheeses and oregano.
6  Bake, covered, in oven, 20 minutes. Uncover; bake about 10 minutes or until browned lightly.

prep + cook time 1 hour  serves 6
nutritional count per serving  27.7g total fat (6.6g saturated fat); 2266kJ (542 cal); 49.4g carbohydrate; 19.9g protein; 8.3g fibre

# creamed corn and potato patties

800g (1½ pounds) potatoes, peeled
1 corn cob (400g), husk and silk removed
2 egg yolks
310g (10 ounces) canned creamed corn
¾ cup (45g) fresh breadcrumbs
¼ cup finely chopped fresh flat-leaf parsley
¼ cup (35g) plain (all-purpose) flour
60g (2 ounces) butter
¼ cup (60ml) vegetable oil

1 Boil, steam or microwave potatoes until tender; drain.
2 Meanwhile, using sharp knife, remove kernels from corn cob.
3 Mash potatoes until smooth. Add corn kernels, egg yolks, creamed corn, breadcrumbs and parsley; stir to combine.
4 Using floured hands, shape mixture into 12 patties. Toss patties in flour, shake away excess. Heat a third of the butter and 1 tablespoon of the oil in large frying pan; cook patties, four at a time, until browned both sides. Repeat until all patties are cooked.

prep + cook time 1 hour  makes 12
nutritional count per patty  9.6g total fat
(3.2g saturated fat); 811kJ (194 cal);
21g carbohydrate; 4.3g protein; 3.1g fibre

# banana chillies with potato and green olive stuffing

30g (1 ounce) butter
2 tablespoons olive oil
3 cloves garlic, crushed
2 teaspoons ground cumin
2 teaspoons dried oregano
600g (1¼ pounds) potatoes, diced into 1cm
  (½ inch) pieces
3 large tomatoes (660g), diced into 1cm
  (½ inch) pieces
1 cup (120g) seeded green olives, chopped coarsely
2 cups (240g) coarsely grated cheddar cheese
8 red or yellow banana chillies (1.3kg)

TOMATO SAUCE
1 tablespoon olive oil
1 clove garlic, crushed
1 medium red onion (170g/5½ ounces), chopped
  coarsely
1 tablespoon ground cumin
2 teaspoons dried oregano
800g (1½ pounds) canned diced tomatoes
½ cup (125ml) water

1  Preheat oven to 180°C/350°F.
2  Heat butter and oil in large frying pan; cook garlic, cumin, oregano and potato, stirring occasionally, about 10 minutes or until potato browns lightly. Add tomato and olives; cook, stirring, about 10 minutes or until liquid has evaporated. Transfer to large bowl; stir in cheese.
3  Meanwhile, using sharp knife, make a small horizontal cut in banana chilli 1cm (½ inch) below stem, then make lengthways slit in chilli, starting from horizontal cut and ending 1cm (½ inch) from tip, taking care not to cut all the way through chilli; discard membrane and seeds. Repeat process with remaining chillies. Carefully divide filling among chillies, securing closed with a toothpick.
4  Make tomato sauce.
5  Place chillies on tomato sauce in dish, cover; bake about 40 minutes or until chillies are tender. Remove toothpicks and serve chillies with tomato sauce.

tomato sauce  Heat oil in large deep flameproof baking dish; cook garlic, onion, cumin and oregano, stirring, until onion softens. Add undrained tomatoes and the water; bring to the boil. Simmer, uncovered, 10 minutes.

prep + cook time 2 hours  serves 4
nutritional count per serving  43.8g total fat (20.3g saturated fat); 2725 kJ (652 calories); 39.9g carbohydrate; 24.4g protein; 11.2g fibre

Serve with a mixed green salad.

# spanish cheese and tomato tortilla

4 green onions (scallions), sliced thickly
1 medium red capsicum (bell pepper) (200g),
  chopped coarsely
2 cloves garlic, crushed
1 fresh long red chilli, chopped finely
2 medium tomatoes (300g), chopped coarsely
200g (6½ ounces) fetta cheese, crumbled
8 eggs
1¼ cups (310ml) pouring cream (see note)
¼ cup firmly packed fresh flat-leaf parsley leaves,
  chopped coarsely

1  Heat oiled 26cm (10½ inch) frying pan; cook
onion, capsicum, garlic and chilli, stirring, until
vegetables are just tender. Remove from heat;
stir in tomato and cheese.
2  Whisk eggs, cream and parsley in large jug.
Pour over capsicum mixture; stir gently.
3  Preheat grill (broiler).
4  Return pan to low heat; cook, uncovered, until
just set. Place pan under grill to brown tortilla top
(protect handle with foil). Cut into wedges to serve.

**prep + cook time** 35 minutes  **serves** 4
**nutritional count per serving**  49.9g total fat
(29g saturated fat); 2424kJ (580 cal);
7.6g carbohydrate; 25.6g protein; 2.2g fibre

**note**  It is fine to use just one 300ml carton of
cream for this recipe.

# baked potatoes with salmon and peas

4 large potatoes (1.2kg), unpeeled
½ cup (60g) frozen peas
60g butter (2 ounces), softened
½ cup (120g) sour cream
100g (3 ounces) smoked salmon, chopped coarsely
2 tablespoons coarsely chopped fresh dill

1  Preheat oven to 180°C/350°F.
2  Pierce potato skins with fork; wrap each potato in foil, place on oven tray. Bake about 1 hour or until tender.
3  Boil, steam or microwave peas until tender; drain.
4  Combine butter and sour cream in medium bowl.
5  Remove potatoes from oven; fold back foil to reveal tops of potatoes.
6  Increase oven temperature to 240°C/475°F.
7  Cut 5mm (¼ inch) from top of each potato; chop coarsely, add to bowl with butter mixture. Carefully scoop out flesh from potatoes, leaving skins intact. Add potato flesh to butter mixture.
8  Mash potato mixture until almost smooth; stir in peas, salmon and dill. Divide among potato shells.
9  Bake potatoes about 10 minutes or until browned lightly and heated through.

prep + cook time 1 hour 30 minutes  serves 4
nutritional count per serving  22.7g total fat
(14.8g saturated fat); 1873kJ (448 cal);
41.1g carbohydrate; 14.6g protein; 6.9g fibre

# mediterranean potato pancakes

1 tablespoon olive oil
1 medium red onion (170g), chopped coarsely
2 cloves garlic, crushed
1 medium red capsicum (bell pepper) (200g),
    chopped coarsely
1 medium yellow capsicum (bell pepper) (200g),
    chopped coarsely
250g (8 ounces) button mushrooms,
    chopped coarsely
¼ cup (60ml) dry red wine
2 medium egg (plum) tomatoes (150g),
    chopped coarsely
2 x 400g (12½ ounces) canned crushed tomatoes
200g (6½ ounces) potatoes, peeled,
    chopped coarsely
¾ cup (110g) plain (all-purpose) flour
¼ teaspoon bicarbonate of soda (baking soda)
2 eggs
1¾ cups (430ml) buttermilk
½ cup coarsely chopped fresh basil
½ cup (40g) coarsely grated parmesan cheese

1  Heat oil in large frying pan; cook onion and garlic, stirring, until onion softens. Add capsicums and mushroom; cook, stirring, until vegetables are just tender. Add wine, fresh tomato and 1 can of the undrained tomatoes; bring to the boil. Simmer, uncovered, about 10 minutes or until mixture thickens slightly.
2  Meanwhile, boil, steam or microwave potato until tender; drain. Mash potato in large bowl; cool 10 minutes.
3  Mix combined sifted flour and soda into potato; gradually whisk in combined eggs and buttermilk until batter is smooth. Refrigerate 10 minutes.
4  Preheat oven to 180°C/350°F.
5  Heat oiled large frying pan; cook ¼-cup of the batter until browned lightly both sides. Repeat to make a total of 12 pancakes. Cool pancakes 10 minutes.
6  Divide vegetable mixture among pancakes; roll to enclose filling. Place 2 pancakes, seam-side down, in each of six 1½-cup (375ml) baking dishes.
7  Combine remaining can of undrained tomatoes and basil in small bowl; pour over pancakes, sprinkle with cheese. Bake, uncovered, about 15 minutes or until heated through.

prep + cook time 1 hour 15 minutes  serves 6
nutritional count per serving  7.5g total fat
(2.8g saturated fat); 1070kJ (256 cal);
30g carbohydrate; 12.6g protein; 5.3g fibre

note  Instead of individual dishes, use a single large shallow 3-litre (12-cup) baking dish for this recipe. The cooking time will be the same.

# tomato, olive and ricotta tart

2 sheets puff pastry
¾ cup (80g) coarsely chopped
  semi-dried tomatoes
¾ cup (90g) seeded black olives
½ cup (120g) crumbled ricotta cheese
½ small red onion (50g), sliced thinly
¼ cup torn fresh basil leaves
1 egg, beaten

**1** Preheat oven to 200°C/400°F. Line oven tray with baking paper (parchment).
**2** Cut 16cm x 24cm (6½ inch x 9½ inch) rectangle from 1 sheet of pastry; place on oven tray. Top with tomatoes, olives, cheese, onion and basil.
**3** Cut 18cm x 24cm (7 inch x 9½ inch) rectangle from another sheet of puff pastry; score pastry in a diamond pattern then place on top of pastry on oven tray, press edges to seal. Brush with egg; bake about 20 minutes.

**prep + cook time** 30 minutes  **serves** 4
**nutritional count per serving**  25.1g total fat
(12.5g saturated fat); 1965kJ (470 cal);
46.9g carbohydrate; 11.5g protein; 5.8g fibre

# spinach and corn pasties

2 medium potatoes (400g)
2 teaspoons vegetable oil
1 small brown onion (80g), chopped finely
250g (8 ounces) thawed, drained, frozen spinach
2 x 310g (10 ounces) canned creamed corn
3 sheets shortcrust pastry
2 tablespoons milk

**1** Cut potatoes into 1cm (½ inch) cubes. Heat oil in large frying pan; cook potato, stirring, until browned lightly. Add onion; cook, stirring, until soft.
**2** Combine potato, onion, spinach and creamed corn in large bowl.
**3** Preheat oven to 200°C/400°F. Oil two oven trays.
**4** Cut each pastry sheet in half diagonally. Divide filling among triangles, placing on one side; fold pastry in half to enclose filling, pressing edges with fork to seal. Place pasties on trays; brush with milk. Bake about 30 minutes or until browned lightly. Serve with sweet chilli sauce, if you like.

**prep + cook time** 1 hour 10 minutes  **serves** 6
**nutritional count per serving** 27.1g total fat (12.6g saturated fat); 2291kJ (548 cal); 62.7g carbohydrate; 9.8g protein; 7.5g fibre

# pulses & grains

## red curry lentils

1 tablespoon olive oil
1 medium brown onion (150g), quartered
2 tablespoons red curry paste
2 x 400g (12½ ounces) canned brown lentils,
  rinsed, drained
1 cup (250ml) vegetable stock
200g (6½ ounces) green beans, halved
2 tablespoons lime juice
⅔ cup (190g) yogurt

1  Heat oil in medium saucepan; cook onion,
stirring, until soft. Add paste; cook, stirring, until
fragrant. Add lentils and stock; bring to the boil.
2  Simmer, uncovered, about 10 minutes or until
stock has thickened. Add beans, simmer 2 minutes.
Remove from heat; stir in juice.
3  Serve curry topped with yogurt.

prep + cook time 20 minutes  serves 4
nutritional count per serving  10.5g total fat
(2.2g saturated fat); 865kJ (207 cal);
14.3g carbohydrate; 11g protein; 6g fibre

# red beans and rice

2 rindless bacon slices (130g), chopped coarsely
1 medium brown onion (150g), chopped finely
1 small red capsicum (bell pepper) (150g),
  chopped finely
2 cloves garlic, crushed
1 tablespoon tomato paste
1 tablespoon red wine vinegar
1 teaspoon smoked paprika
2 cups (400g) white long-grain rice
1 bay leaf
1 cup (250ml) chicken stock
2¼ cups (560ml) water
400g (12½ ounces) canned kidney beans,
  rinsed, drained
½ cup (80g) frozen corn kernels
1 tablespoon lime juice

**1** Cook bacon in heated large frying pan, stirring,
until starting to crisp. Add onion, capsicum and
garlic; cook, stirring until capsicum softens.
**2** Add paste, vinegar and paprika; cook, stirring,
1 minute. Add rice; cook, stirring, 2 minutes.
**3** Add bay leaf, stock, the water and beans to pan;
bring to the boil. Simmer, covered, 20 minutes.
Add corn; cook, covered, about 5 minutes or until
rice is tender. Remove from heat; stand, covered,
5 minutes. Stir in juice.

**prep + cook time** 1 hour  **serves** 4
**nutritional count per serving** 3.3g total fat
(1g saturated fat); 2215kJ (530 cal);
99.3g carbohydrate; 20.8g protein; 7.1g fibre

# chicken, pea and broad bean risotto

1 litre (4 cups) chicken stock
1 cup (250ml) water
60g (2 ounces) butter
600g (1¼ pounds) chicken tenderloins, sliced thickly
4 green onions (scallions), sliced thinly
1 clove garlic, crushed
1½ cups (300g) arborio rice
1 cup (150g) frozen broad (fava) beans, thawed
1 cup (120g) frozen peas, thawed
1 cup (80g) finely grated parmesan cheese
1 tablespoon finely chopped fresh mint

1  Place stock and the water in medium saucepan; bring to the boil, then simmer, covered.
2  Heat half the butter in large saucepan; cook chicken, in batches, until just browned. Remove from pan.
3  Heat remaining butter in same pan; cook onion and garlic, stirring, until soft. Add rice; stir to coat in onion mixture. Add ½ cup of the simmering stock mixture; cook, stirring, over low heat until stock is absorbed. Continue adding stock, in ½-cup batches, stirring, until stock is absorbed after each addition. Return chicken to pan halfway through cooking time. Total cooking time should be about 35 minutes or until rice is tender.
4  Meanwhile, pour boiling water over beans; stand 2 minutes. Drain; peel away grey-coloured outer shells.
5  Add peas and beans to risotto, stir gently until hot. Remove from heat; stir in cheese and mint.

prep + cook time 55 minutes  serves 4
nutritional count per serving 24.7g total fat (13.3g saturated fat); 2951kJ (706 cal); 67.3g carbohydrate; 50.5g protein; 5.9g fibre

Serve with a mixed leaf, parsley and mint salad.

57

# felafel

2 x 400g (12½ ounces) canned chickpeas
  (garbanzo), rinsed, drained
1 clove garlic, chopped coarsely
1 small brown onion (80g), chopped coarsely
1 tablespoon olive oil
1 egg
2 teaspoons ground cumin
½ teaspoon bicarbonate of soda (baking soda)
2 tablespoons plain (all-purpose) flour
vegetable oil, for shallow-frying
4 large pitta breads (320g), warmed

YOGURT SAUCE
1 cup (280g) yogurt
½ clove garlic, crushed
1 tablespoon lemon juice
½ teaspoon cayenne pepper

1  To make felafel mixture, process chickpeas,
garlic, onion and olive oil until ingredients begin to
combine; transfer mixture to medium bowl. Stir in
egg, cumin, soda and flour until combined. Shape
mixture into 12 patties.
2  Heat vegetable oil in large frying pan; cook
felafel, in batches, until browned. Remove from
pan. Drain on absorbent paper.
3  Meanwhile, make yogurt sauce.
4  Serve felafel on pitta, topped with yogurt sauce.

**yogurt sauce**  Combine ingredients in small bowl.

**prep + cook time** 25 minutes  **serves** 4
**nutritional count per serving**  21.8g total fat
(4.3g saturated fat); 2416kJ (575 cal);
68.3g carbohydrate; 21.7g protein; 9.1g fibre

**Serve with** a rocket (arugula) and tomato salad.

# nasi goreng

1 tablespoon peanut oil
2 eggs, beaten lightly
1 teaspoon sesame oil
1 medium brown onion (150g), sliced thinly
4 green onions (scallions), sliced thinly
1 clove garlic, crushed
5cm (2 inch) piece fresh ginger (25g), grated
2 cups (160g) shredded wombok
1 cup (80g) bean sprouts
3 cups (450g) cooked white long-grain rice
1 tablespoon sambal oelek
1 tablespoon kecap manis
1 lebanese cucumber (130g), sliced thinly
1 medium tomato (150g), sliced thinly

1  Heat one teaspoon of the peanut oil in large wok; add half the egg mixture, swirl wok to make a thin omelette. Remove omelette from wok; roll into cigar-shape, cut into thin strips. Repeat with one more teaspoon of the peanut oil and remaining egg mixture.
2  Heat remaining peanut oil and sesame oil in wok; stir-fry onions, garlic and ginger until onion softens. Add cabbage and sprouts; stir-fry over high heat until vegetables are just tender.
3  Add rice, omelette, sambal and kecap manis to wok; stir-fry until heated through.
4  Serve nasi goreng with cucumber and tomato.

**prep + cook time** 40 minutes  **serves** 4
**nutritional count per serving**  8.9g total fat
(1.8g saturated fat); 1292kJ (302 cal);
45.6g carbohydrate; 9.3g protein; 4.1g fibre

**note** You need to cook 1½ cups (300g) white rice to get the amount of cooked rice needed for this recipe.

# jambalaya

1 tablespoon olive oil
4 smoked chorizo sausages (680g)
400g (12½ ounces) chicken breast fillets
1 medium red onion (170g), chopped finely
1 medium red capsicum (bell pepper) (200g),
  chopped finely
2 cloves garlic, crushed
2 tablespoons finely chopped bottled
  jalapeño chillies
1 teaspoon dried oregano
¼ teaspoon cayenne pepper
1 bay leaf
2 tablespoons tomato paste
1½ cups (300g) white long-grain rice
400g (12½ ounces) canned crushed tomatoes
2 cups (500ml) chicken stock

1  Heat oil in large saucepan; cook sausages,
turning occasionally, until browned. Remove from
pan; slice thickly.
2  Add chicken to pan; cook, turning occasionally,
until browned. Remove from pan; slice thickly.
3  Cook onion, capsicum and garlic in same pan,
stirring, until capsicum softens. Add chilli; cook,
stirring, 1 minute. Add spices, bay leaf and paste;
cook, stirring, 2 minutes. Add rice; stir to coat
in mixture.
4  Add undrained tomatoes and stock, bring to a
simmer; return sausage and chicken to pan. Cook,
covered, about 45 minutes or until rice is tender
and liquid absorbed.

prep + cook time 1 hour 30 minutes  serves 4
nutritional count per serving  62.3g total fat
(21.2g saturated fat); 4648kJ (1112 cal);
73g carbohydrate; 63.3g protein; 4.5g fibre

# vegetarian paella

2 cups (500ml) vegetable stock
3 cups (750ml) water
1 tablespoon olive oil
2 cloves garlic, crushed
1 medium red onion (170g), chopped finely
2 medium tomatoes (300g), seeded, chopped finely
1 medium red capsicum (bell pepper) (200g),
 chopped finely
¼ teaspoon ground turmeric
2 teaspoons smoked sweet paprika
1¾ cups (350g) arborio rice
1 cup (120g) frozen peas
100g (3 ounces) frozen baby beans
¼ cup (30g) seeded black olives, sliced
⅓ cup finely chopped fresh flat-leaf parsley

**1** Combine stock and the water in medium
saucepan; bring to the boil. Remove from heat.
**2** Heat oil in large frying pan; cook garlic, onion,
tomato, capsicum, turmeric and paprika, stirring,
until vegetables soften. Add rice; stir to coat in
mixture. Stir in stock mixture; bring to the boil.
Simmer, uncovered, about 20 minutes or until rice
is almost tender.
**3** Sprinkle peas and beans evenly over surface
of paella; simmer, covered, about 5 minutes or
until rice is tender. Add olives and parsley; stand,
covered, 5 minutes.

**prep + cook time** 1 hour  **serves** 4
**nutritional count per serving**  6g total fat
(1g saturated fat); 1818kJ (435 cal);
79.7g carbohydrate; 11.5g protein; 5.7g fibre

# chickpea vegetable braise with cumin couscous

1 cup (200g) dried chickpeas (garbanzo)
2 tablespoons olive oil
2 small leeks (400g), chopped coarsely
2 medium carrots (240g), cut into batons
2 cloves garlic, crushed
1 tablespoon finely chopped fresh rosemary
2 tablespoons white wine vinegar
2 cups (500ml) vegetable stock
100g (3 ounces) baby spinach leaves
¼ cup (60ml) lemon juice
2 tablespoons olive oil, extra
2 cloves garlic, crushed, extra

CUMIN COUSCOUS
1 cup (250ml) boiling water
1 cup (200g) couscous
1 tablespoon olive oil
1 teaspoon ground cumin

TOMATO AND RED ONION SALAD
4 medium tomatoes (600g), sliced thinly
2 medium red onions (340g), sliced thinly
2 tablespoons red wine vinegar
1 tablespoon olive oil

1 Place chickpeas in medium bowl, cover with cold water; stand overnight, drain. Rinse under cold water; drain. Place chickpeas in medium saucepan of boiling water. Return to the boil, then simmer, uncovered, about 40 minutes or until chickpeas are tender. Drain.
2 Meanwhile, preheat oven to 170°C/325°F.
3 Heat oil in large deep flameproof baking dish; cook leek and carrot, on stove top, stirring, until just tender. Add garlic, rosemary and chickpeas; cook, stirring, until fragrant. Add vinegar and stock; bring to the boil. Cover dish, transfer to oven; roast, 30 minutes.
4 Make cumin couscous; make tomato and red onion salad.
5 Remove dish from oven; stir in spinach, juice, extra oil and extra garlic. Serve vegetable braise with couscous and tomato and red onion salad.

cumin couscous Combine the water and couscous in medium heatproof bowl, cover; stand about 5 minutes or until liquid is absorbed, fluffing with fork occasionally. Add oil and cumin; toss gently to combine.

tomato and red onion salad Arrange tomato and onion on serving platter; drizzle with combined vinegar and oil. Sprinkle with cracked black pepper to serve.

prep + cook time 1 hour 45 minutes (+ standing)
serves 4
nutritional count per serving 31.6g total fat (4.6g saturated fat); 2717kJ (650 cal); 68.7g carbohydrate; 21.3g protein; 13.8g fibre

# lentil cottage pie

4 medium potatoes (800g/1½ pounds),
  chopped coarsely
½ cup (125ml) milk, warmed
4 green onions (scallions), chopped finely
½ cup (100g) french-style green lentils
1 tablespoon olive oil
1 large brown onion (200g), chopped finely
1 medium red capsicum (bell pepper) (200g),
  chopped coarsely
2 medium zucchini (240g), chopped coarsely
1 medium eggplant (300g), chopped coarsely
2 cloves garlic, crushed
400g (12½ ounces) canned crushed tomatoes

1  Boil, steam or microwave potato until tender;
drain. Mash potato with milk and green onion
until smooth.
2  Meanwhile, cook lentils in small saucepan of
boiling water until just tender; drain. Rinse; drain.
3  Preheat oven to 200°C/400°F.
4  Heat oil in medium saucepan; cook brown
onion, capsicum, zucchini, eggplant and garlic,
stirring, until vegetables soften. Add lentils and
undrained tomato; bring to the boil. Simmer
about 10 minutes or until mixture has thickened.
5  Spoon mixture into oiled shallow 2.5 litre
(10-cup) baking dish; spread with potato. Bake,
uncovered, in oven, about 30 minutes or until
top browns lightly.

**prep + cook time** 1 hour 35 minutes  **serves** 4
**nutritional count per serving**  7.3g total fat
(1.5g saturated fat); 1384kJ (331 cal);
44.8g carbohydrate; 15.4g protein; 11.8g fibre

# chicken, lentil and cauliflower pilaf

1 medium brown onion (150g), sliced thinly
1 clove garlic, crushed
2 tablespoons madras curry paste
1 cup (200g) basmati rice
½ small cauliflower (500g), cut into florets
400g (12½ ounces) canned brown lentils,
  rinsed, drained
1 cup (250ml) chicken stock
1 cup (250ml) water
2 cups (320g) coarsely chopped barbecued chicken
½ cup firmly packed fresh coriander
  (cilantro) leaves

1   Cook onion and garlic in heated oiled large
frying pan until onion softens. Add paste; cook,
stirring, about 5 minutes or until fragrant.
2   Add rice, cauliflower and lentils; stir to coat in
onion mixture. Add stock, the water and chicken;
bring to the boil. Simmer, covered tightly, about
15 minutes or until rice is tender and liquid has
been absorbed. Remove from heat; fluff with fork.
Stir in coriander.

**prep + cook time** 30 minutes  **serves** 4
**nutritional count per serving**  10.7g total fat (2.3g
saturated fat); 1814kJ (434 cal); 50.2g carbohydrate;
36.6g protein; 6.1g fibre

**note**  You need to buy a barbecued chicken
weighing approximately 900g (1¾ pounds) to get
the amount of chicken required for this recipe.

**Serve with** lime wedges, pappadums and
mango chutney.

# risotto terrine

1 medium green capsicum (bell pepper) (200g)
1 medium red capsicum (bell pepper) (200g)
8 medium egg (plum) tomatoes (600g), halved
3½ cups (875ml) vegetable stock
1 tablespoon olive oil
1 medium brown onion (150g), chopped finely
1 clove garlic, crushed
1½ cups (300g) arborio rice
½ cup (125ml) dry white wine
20g low-fat dairy-free spread
½ cup (40g) coarsely grated parmesan cheese
60g (2 ounces) baby spinach leaves

1  Preheat oven to 180°C/350°F.
2  Quarter capsicums; discard seeds and membranes. Place capsicum and tomato on oven tray; roast, uncovered, skin-side up, about 40 minutes or until capsicum and tomato soften. Cover capsicum pieces with plastic or paper 5 minutes then peel away skin.
3  Meanwhile, place stock in medium saucepan; bring to the boil, then simmer, covered.
4  Heat oil in large saucepan; cook onion and garlic, stirring, until onion softens. Add rice; stir to coat rice in onion mixture. Add wine; cook, stirring, until wine is absorbed. Add ½ cup of the simmering stock; cook, stirring, over low heat, until stock is absorbed. Continue adding stock, in ½-cup batches, stirring, until stock is absorbed after each addition. Total cooking time should be about 35 minutes or until rice is tender. Stir in spread and cheese. Cool to room temperature.
5  Line 10cm x 25cm (4 inch x 10 inch) terrine dish with plastic wrap. Layer half the tomato, cut-side down, then half the spinach, half the risotto, all the capsicum, remaining tomato, remaining spinach and remaining risotto. Cover terrine; weight with another dish filled with heavy cans. Refrigerate 3 hours or overnight. Bring terrine to room temperature before serving.

**prep + cook time** 1 hour 10 minutes
(+ cooling, refrigeration and standing)  **serves** 6
**nutritional count per serving** 7.6g total fat
(2.4g saturated fat); 1292kJ (309 cal);
46.1g carbohydrate; 10.1g protein; 3.1g fibre

# soups

## lentil and garlic soup with yogurt

Heat 1 tablespoon olive oil in large saucepan; cook
10 thinly sliced garlic cloves and 2 sprigs fresh thyme,
stirring, until garlic softens. Stir in 2 cups french-style
green lentils then 2 cups vegetable stock and 2 litres
(8 cups) water; bring to the boil. Simmer, covered,
about 35 minutes or until lentils soften; cool soup
10 minutes. Meanwhile, combine 1 cup yogurt,
1 tablespoon lemon juice and ¼ cup finely chopped
fresh mint in small bowl. Blend or process soup, in
batches, until pureed; return to pan. Add 1½ cups
firmly packed trimmed watercress to soup; cook,
stirring, until wilted. Serve soup with minted yogurt.

**prep + cook time** 55 minutes **serves** 6
**nutritional count per serving** 6.5g total fat
(1.9g saturated fat); 1158kJ (277 cal);
28.9g carbohydrate; 20.1g protein; 16.7g fibre

## pea and ham soup

Combine 1 coarsely chopped medium brown onion,
2 trimmed, coarsely chopped celery stalks, 2 bay
leaves, 1.5kg (3 pounds) ham hocks, 2.5 litres (10 cups)
water and 1 teaspoon cracked black pepper in large
saucepan; bring to the boil. Reduce heat; simmer,
covered, about 1½ hours. Add 2 cups split green
peas; simmer, covered, 30 minutes or until peas are
tender. Cool soup 10 minutes. Remove hocks from
pan; when cool enough to handle, remove meat
from hocks. Shred meat finely. Discard bones, fat
and skin; remove and discard bay leaves. Blend or
process half the soup mixture, in batches, until
smooth. Return to pan with remaining soup mixture
and ham; stir soup until heated through.

**prep + cook time** 2 hours 15 minutes **serves** 6
**nutritional count per serving** 4.9g total fat
(1.4g saturated fat); 1162kJ (278 cal);
31g carbohydrate; 23.5g protein; 7.3g fibre

## white bean, chickpea and risoni soup

Heat 1 tablespoon olive oil in large saucepan; cook 1 coarsely chopped medium brown onion and 1 coarsely chopped large carrot, stirring, until carrot softens. Add 2 thinly sliced garlic cloves, 2 tablespoons tomato paste and 2 teaspoons ground cumin; cook, stirring, until garlic softens. Add 2 x 400g (12½ ounces) canned crushed tomatoes and 1 litre (4 cups) vegetable stock to pan; bring to the boil. Add 400g (12½ ounces) canned rinsed, drained chickpeas (garbanzo) and 400g (12½ ounces) canned rinsed, drained white beans; return to the boil. Add ⅓ cup risoni pasta; boil about 10 minutes or until risoni is tender.

**prep + cook time** 45 minutes **serves** 4
**nutritional count per serving** 7.8g total fat (1.4g saturated fat); 1359kJ (325 cal); 41.9g carbohydrate; 15.5g protein; 11.6g fibre

## harira

Cook ½ cup french-style green lentils, 500g (1 pound) finely diced lamb, 1 finely chopped medium brown onion, 2 crushed garlic cloves, ½ teaspoon each ground cinnamon, ginger and hot paprika, pinch saffron threads and 1 teaspoon ground turmeric in large flameproof casserole dish, stirring, until lamb is browned. Add 1.5 litres (6 cups) water; bring to the boil. Simmer, covered, 1 hour. Add 400g (12½ ounces) canned rinsed, drained chickpeas (garbanzo), ½ cup white long-grain rice and 3 finely chopped small egg (plum) tomatoes to dish; simmer, uncovered, about 20 minutes or until rice is just tender. Stir in ¼ cup finely chopped fresh flat-leaf parsley.

**prep + cook time** 1 hour 40 minutes **serves** 4
**nutritional count per serving** 13.1g total fat (5.3g saturated fat); 1919kJ (459 cal); 41.4g carbohydrate; 39.1g protein; 8.3g fibre

# pasta

## beef, garlic and silver beet pasta bake

250g (8 ounces) small macaroni pasta
2 teaspoons vegetable oil
4 cloves garlic, crushed
250g (8 ounces) trimmed silver beet (swiss chard), finely shredded
300g (9½ ounces) sour cream
½ cup (60g) coarsely grated cheddar cheese

BOLOGNESE
½ tablespoon olive oil
1 large brown onion (200g), chopped finely
2 cloves garlic, crushed
600g (1¼ pounds) minced (ground) beef
1 large carrot (180g), grated coarsely
2 tablespoons tomato paste
1½ cups (375ml) beef stock
810g (1½ pounds) canned crushed tomatoes
½ tablespoon mixed dried herbs

1  Make bolognese.
2  Preheat oven to 200°C/400°F.
3  Cook pasta in large saucepan of boiling water until just tender; drain.
4  Meanwhile, heat oil in large frying pan; cook garlic, stirring, 1 minute. Add silver beet; cook, stirring, until wilted. Stir in pasta and sour cream.

5  Spread half the bolognese into shallow 3-litre (12-cup) baking dish. Layer with half the silver beet mixture; top with remaining bolognese then remaining silver beet mixture. Sprinkle cheese over mixture.
6  Bake, uncovered, in oven, about 20 minutes or until browned and heated through.

bolognese  Heat oil in medium saucepan; cook onion and garlic, stirring, until onion softens. Add mince; cook, stirring, until browned. Add carrot and paste; cook, stirring, 5 minutes. Add stock, undrained tomato and herbs; bring to the boil, then simmer, covered, 45 minutes, stirring occasionally. Uncover; simmer, about 45 minutes or until thickened slightly.

prep + cook time 2 hours 45 minutes  serves 6
nutritional count per serving  38.2g total fat (20.5g saturated fat); 2654kJ (635 cal); 38.7g carbohydrate; 31.7g protein; 6g fibre

# baked penne with kumara and spinach

2 medium red onions (340g), cut into wedges
2 small kumara (orange sweet potato) (600g),
 sliced thickly
2 tablespoons olive oil
375g (12 ounces) penne pasta
250g (8 ounces) frozen spinach, thawed, drained
1½ cups (360g) ricotta cheese
1 clove garlic, crushed
¼ cup (60ml) pouring cream
2 x 400g (12½ ounces) canned crushed tomatoes
¼ cup (40g) pine nuts
½ cup (40g) finely grated parmesan cheese

1  Preheat oven to 220°C/425°F.
2  Combine onion and kumara with oil in large
baking dish; roast, uncovered, stirring once, about
40 minutes or until tender.
3  Cook pasta in large saucepan of boiling water
until tender; drain.
4  Combine pasta in large bowl with spinach, ricotta,
garlic, cream and tomatoes.
5  Spread kumara mixture over base of 3-litre (12-cup)
baking dish. Top with pasta mixture; sprinkle with nuts
and parmesan. Bake, covered, 10 minutes. Uncover;
bake about 5 minutes or until browned lightly.

**prep + cook time** 1 hour 10 minutes  **serves** 6
**nutritional count per serving**  25.3g total fat
(9.8g saturated fat); 2450kJ (586 cal);
63.4g carbohydrate; 21.9g protein; 8.4g fibre

# penne bolognese

2 tablespoons olive oil
1 small brown onion (80g), chopped finely
1 medium carrot (120g), chopped finely
1 stalk celery (150g), trimmed, chopped finely
2 cloves garlic, sliced thinly
500g (1 pound) minced (ground) beef
500g (1 pound) minced (ground) pork
½ cup (125ml) milk
½ cup (125ml) dry red wine
2 x 400g (12½ ounces) canned crushed tomatoes
1 cup (250ml) beef stock
500g (1 pound) penne pasta

1  Heat oil in large saucepan, add onion, carrot, celery and garlic; cook, stirring, until celery softens.
2  Add both minces to pan; cook, stirring, until browned. Add milk and wine; simmer, uncovered, until liquid is almost evaporated.
3  Add undrained tomatoes to pan; cook, stirring, 5 minutes. Add stock; bring to the boil. Simmer, covered, 30 minutes.
4  Meanwhile, cook pasta in large saucepan of boiling water until tender; drain. Combine sauce mixture with pasta; sprinkle with grated parmesan cheese to serve.

**prep + cook time** 1 hour  **serves** 6
**nutritional count per serving**  19.8g total fat
(6.2g saturated fat); 2700kJ (646 cal);
64.4g carbohydrate; 45.7g protein; 5.6g fibre

# pea and salmon pasta bake

375g (12 ounces) rigatoni pasta
30g (1 ounce) butter
2 tablespoons plain (all-purpose) flour
2 cups (500ml) milk
1½ cups (180g) frozen peas
½ cup (40g) coarsely grated parmesan cheese
1¼ cups (150g) coarsely grated cheddar cheese
415g (13 ounces) canned pink salmon, drained,
  skin and bones removed

1  Preheat oven to 200°C/400°F.
2  Cook pasta in large saucepan of boiling water
until tender; drain.
3  Meanwhile, melt butter in medium saucepan.
Add flour; cook, stirring, until mixture thickens and
bubbles. Gradually stir in milk; stir over medium heat
until sauce boils and thickens. Stir in peas, ¼ cup
parmesan and ¾ cup cheddar.
4  Combine sauce mixture with pasta and salmon
in oiled shallow 2.5-litre (10-cup) ovenproof dish;
sprinkle with remaining combined cheeses. Bake,
uncovered, in oven, about 20 minutes or until
browned lightly.

**prep + cook time** 50 minutes  **serves** 6
**nutritional count per serving**  23.8g total fat
(13.7g saturated fat); 2345kJ (561 cal);
51.2g carbohydrate; 33.1g protein; 3.9g fibre

# penne with char-grilled capsicum and pine nuts

2 large red capsicums (bell peppers) (700g)
375g (12 ounces) penne pasta
2 tablespoons olive oil
2 cloves garlic, crushed
½ cup (80g) roasted pine nuts
2 fresh small red thai chillies (serrano),
  chopped finely
¼ cup (60ml) lemon juice
100g (3 ounces) baby rocket leaves (arugula)
100g (3 ounces) fetta cheese, crumbled

1  Quarter capsicums; discard seeds and membranes.
Roast under very hot grill (broiler), skin-side up,
until skin blisters and blackens. Cover capsicum
pieces in plastic or paper for 5 minutes; peel away
skin then slice thinly.
2  Cook pasta in large saucepan of boiling water
until just tender; drain.
3  Meanwhile, heat oil in large frying pan; cook
garlic, nuts and chilli, stirring, about 2 minutes or
until fragrant. Add capsicum and juice; stir until hot.
4  Place pasta and capsicum mixture in large bowl
with rocket and cheese; toss gently to combine.

prep + cook time 35 minutes  serves 4
nutritional count per serving  30.5g total fat
(6.2g saturated fat); 2755kJ (659 cal);
74.4g carbohydrate; 21g protein; 8.2g fibre

# ravioli with tomato, pea and basil sauce

2 teaspoons olive oil
6 slices pancetta (90g)
1 clove garlic, crushed
700g (1½ pounds) bottled tomato pasta sauce
¼ cup (60ml) dry white wine
2 tablespoons finely chopped fresh basil
1 cup (120g) frozen peas
625g (1¼ pounds) spinach and ricotta ravioli

**1** Heat oil in large frying pan; cook pancetta until crisp. Drain on absorbent paper; break into pieces.
**2** Cook garlic in same pan, stirring, 1 minute. Add sauce, wine and basil; bring to the boil. Add peas; simmer, uncovered, 15 minutes.
**3** Meanwhile, cook ravioli in large saucepan of boiling water until just tender; drain. Return ravioli to pan, add sauce; toss to combine. Divide among serving bowls; top with pancetta.

**prep + cook time** 25 minutes  **serves** 4
**nutritional count per serving** 12.8g total fat
(4.1g saturated fat); 1593kJ (381 cal);
46.6g carbohydrate; 20.1g protein; 7.4g fibre

# creamy chicken, mushroom and asparagus bake

375g (12 ounces) rigatoni pasta
60g (2 ounces) butter
600g (1¼ pounds) chicken breast fillets, diced
  into 1cm (½ inch) pieces
100g (3 ounces) button mushrooms, sliced thinly
2 tablespoons plain (all-purpose) flour
2 cups (500ml) milk
½ cup (40g) coarsely grated romano cheese
1¼ cups (150g) coarsely grated cheddar cheese
170g (5½ ounces) asparagus, trimmed,
  chopped coarsely
¼ cup coarsely chopped fresh flat-leaf parsley

1  Preheat oven to 200°C/400°F.
2  Cook pasta in large saucepan of boiling water
until just tender; drain.
3  Meanwhile, heat a third of the butter in large
frying pan; cook chicken, in batches, until browned
and cooked through. Remove from pan.
4  Heat remaining butter in pan; cook mushrooms,
stirring, until tender. Add flour; cook, stirring,
1 minute. Gradually stir in milk. Stir over medium
heat until mixture boils and thickens. Stir in chicken,
¼ cup of the romano, ¾ cup of the cheddar and
the asparagus.
5  Combine chicken mixture and drained pasta in
2.5-litre (10-cup) ovenproof dish; sprinkle with
remaining cheeses. Cook, uncovered, in oven,
about 15 minutes or until top browns lightly. Serve
pasta bake sprinkled with parsley.

prep + cook time 50 minutes  serves 4
nutritional count per serving  37.3g total fat
(22.3g saturated fat); 3775kJ (903 cal);
75.2g carbohydrate; 64g protein; 4.8g fibre

# chicken, spinach and ricotta bake

1 tablespoon olive oil
1 large brown onion (200g), chopped finely
2 cloves garlic, crushed
10 instant lasagne sheets (200g)
1½ cups (240g) shredded barbecue chicken
1 cup (100g) coarsely grated pizza cheese
3 cups (750ml) bottled tomato pasta sauce
2 cups (500ml) water
50g (1½ ounces) baby spinach leaves
½ cup (120g) firm ricotta cheese, crumbled

1  Heat oil in shallow flameproof dish; cook onion and garlic, on stove top, stirring, until onion softens.
2  Meanwhile, break lasagne sheets into bite-sized pieces. Sprinkle pasta pieces, chicken and half the pizza cheese into the dish.
3  Pour combined pasta sauce and the water over top of chicken mixture. Simmer, covered, about 20 minutes or until pasta is tender.
4  Meanwhile, preheat grill (broiler).
5  Sprinkle bake with spinach, ricotta and remaining pizza cheese; grill about 5 minutes or until cheese melts. Stand, covered, 10 minutes before serving.

**prep + cook time** 50 minutes  **serves** 4
**nutritional count per serving**  18.8g total fat (7.7g saturated fat); 2195kJ (525 cal); 49.7g carbohydrate; 34.9g protein; 6.9g fibre

**note**  You need half a large barbecued chicken weighing 450g (14½ ounces) for this recipe.

# chickpea, preserved lemon and risoni salad

250g (8 ounces) frozen peas
1¼ cups (275g) risoni pasta
1 tablespoon olive oil
2 cloves garlic, crushed
1 celery stalk (150g), trimmed, chopped finely
400g (12½ ounces) canned chickpeas (garbanzo),
  rinsed, drained
2 pieces preserved lemon rind (70g), trimmed,
  chopped finely
⅓ cup (55g) seeded black olives
115g goat's cheese, crumbled

YOGURT DRESSING
⅓ cup (95g) yogurt
1 tablespoon white wine vinegar

1  Boil, steam or microwave peas until tender.
2  Meanwhile, make yogurt dressing.
3  Cook risoni in medium saucepan of boiling
water until tender; drain.
4  Meanwhile, heat oil in large frying pan; cook
garlic and celery, stirring, until celery softens
slightly. Stir in chickpeas, preserved rind, olives,
risoni and peas. Sprinkle cheese over salad; drizzle
with dressing.
**yogurt dressing** Whisk ingredients in small bowl
until combined.

**prep + cook time** 35 minutes  **serves** 4
**nutritional count per serving**  13.4g total fat
(5.1g saturated fat); 2052kJ (491 cal);
66g carbohydrate; 21g protein; 10.4g fibre

# spinach and herb cannelloni

1kg (2 pounds) spinach, trimmed, chopped coarsely
500g (1 pound) ricotta cheese
2 eggs
1½ cups (120g) coarsely grated parmesan cheese
¼ cup finely chopped fresh mint
3 teaspoons finely chopped fresh thyme
2 teaspoons finely chopped fresh rosemary
250g (8 ounces) cannelloni tubes

CREAMY TOMATO SAUCE
1 tablespoon olive oil
1 medium brown onion (150g), chopped finely
4 cloves garlic, crushed
4 x 400g (12½ ounces) canned diced tomatoes
½ cup (125ml) pouring cream
1 teaspoon white sugar

1 Make creamy tomato sauce.
2 Meanwhile, preheat oven to 180°C/350°F.
3 Cook washed, drained spinach in heated large saucepan, stirring, until wilted. Drain; when cool enough to handle, squeeze out excess moisture.
4 Combine spinach in large bowl with ricotta, eggs, ½ cup of the parmesan and the herbs. Using a large piping bag, fill pasta with spinach mixture.
5 Spread a third of the sauce into shallow 25cm x 35cm (10 inch x 14 inch) ovenproof dish; top with pasta, in single layer, then top with remaining sauce. Cook, covered, in oven, 20 minutes. Uncover, sprinkle pasta with remaining parmesan; cook about 15 minutes or until pasta is tender and cheese is browned lightly.

creamy tomato sauce Heat oil in large saucepan; cook onion, stirring, until softened. Add garlic; cook, stirring, until fragrant. Add undrained tomatoes; bring to the boil. Simmer mixture, uncovered, stirring occasionally, about 20 minutes or until sauce thickens slightly. Cool 10 minutes; blend or process sauce with cream and sugar until smooth.

prep + cook time 1 hour serves 6
nutritional count per serving 31g total fat (17.1g saturated fat); 2412kJ (577 cal); 41.8g carbohydrate; 28.7g protein; 8.3g fibre

# fast pasta

## pumpkin and sage ravioli

Cut a 600g (1¼ pound) piece pumpkin into 1cm
(½ inch) cubes. Cook ¼ cup pine nuts in large frying
pan, stirring, until browned lightly; remove from pan.
Heat 2 teaspoons olive oil in pan; cook 3 crushed
garlic cloves and the pumpkin, covered, stirring
occasionally, about 10 minutes or until pumpkin is
almost tender. Meanwhile, cook 625g (1¼ pounds)
ricotta ravioli in large saucepan of boiling water until
just tender; drain. Add nuts, 1¼ cups pouring cream
(or one 300ml carton), ¼ cup finely grated parmesan
cheese and 2 tablespoons coarsely chopped fresh
sage to the pumpkin mixture; bring to the boil.
Reduce heat; simmer, uncovered, 5 minutes. Add
ravioli and 2 tablespoons lemon juice; stir until hot.

**prep + cook time** 25 minutes **serves** 4
**nutritional count per serving** 51.7g total fat
(26.7g saturated fat); 2826kJ (676 cal);
32.5g carbohydrate; 19.2g protein; 4.7g fibre

## spaghetti with pesto

Blend or process 2 coarsely chopped garlic cloves,
⅓ cup roasted pine nuts, ½ cup finely grated
parmesan cheese and 2 cups firmly packed fresh
basil leaves until almost smooth. Gradually add
½ cup olive oil in a thin, steady stream, processing
until thick. Cook 500g (1 pound) spaghetti in large
saucepan of boiling water, until just tender; drain,
reserving ¼ cup of the cooking liquid. Combine
pasta, pesto and reserved cooking liquid in large
bowl. Sprinkle over ½ cup flaked parmesan cheese
to serve.

**prep + cook time** 25 minutes **serves** 4
**nutritional count per serving** 45.2g total fat
(8.9g saturated fat); 3578kJ (859 cal);
86.2g carbohydrate; 23.6g protein; 5.6g fibre

## gnocchi formaggio

Cook 500g (1 pound) potato gnocchi in large saucepan of boiling water until gnocchi float to the surface; drain. Meanwhile, bring 1 cup pouring cream to the boil in small saucepan. Simmer, uncovered, 3 minutes or until reduced by half. Remove cream from heat; gradually stir in 50g (1½ ounces) coarsely crumbled gorgonzola cheese, ⅔ cup coarsely grated pecorino cheese and ⅔ cup coarsely grated parmesan cheese until smooth. Return gnocchi to saucepan with cheese sauce and ¼ cup coarsely chopped garlic chives; stir gently to combine.

**prep + cook time** 20 minutes **serves** 4
**nutritional count per serving** 39.7g total fat (25.7g saturated fat); 2433kJ (582 cal); 38.3g carbohydrate; 17.3g protein; 3g fibre

## tuna and chilli pasta

Cook 375g (12 ounces) angel hair pasta in large saucepan of boiling water until tender; drain, reserving ¼ cup cooking liquid. Rinse pasta under cold water, drain. Meanwhile, drain 425g (13½ ounces) canned tuna in oil, reserving 2 tablespoons of the oil. Heat oil in medium frying pan, add 4 thinly sliced garlic cloves; cook, stirring, until fragrant. Add 1 teaspoon dried chilli flakes and ⅓ cup dry white wine; cook, uncovered, stirring occasionally, until liquid is almost evaporated. Add 400g (12½ ounces) undrained canned chopped tomatoes, tuna and reserved cooking liquid to pan; simmer until liquid has reduced slightly. Remove from heat; stir in 1 tablespoon lemon juice. Combine pasta and sauce in large bowl.

**prep + cook time** 15 minutes **serves** 4
**nutritional count per serving** 22.3g total fat (3.2g saturated fat); 2617kJ (626 cal); 67.5g carbohydrate; 32.5g protein; 4.8g fibre

# stews & curries

## green curry with chicken meatballs

800g (1½ pounds) minced (ground) chicken
2 cloves garlic, crushed
2cm (¾ inch) piece fresh ginger (10g), grated
2 tablespoons finely chopped fresh
  coriander (cilantro)
2 tablespoons peanut oil
¼ cup (75g) green curry paste
3⅓ cups (800ml) canned coconut cream
2 tablespoons fish sauce
2 tablespoons lime juice
1 tablespoon grated palm sugar
150g (4½ ounces) sugar snap peas, trimmed
1 cup (80g) bean sprouts
⅓ cup loosely packed fresh coriander
  (cilantro) leaves
⅔ cup (100g) roasted unsalted cashews
1 fresh long green chilli, sliced thinly

1  Combine chicken, garlic, ginger and chopped coriander in large bowl; roll level tablespoons of mixture into balls.
2  Heat half the oil in large frying pan; cook chicken meatballs until browned.
3  Meanwhile, heat remaining oil in large saucepan; cook paste, stirring, about 2 minutes or until fragrant. Add coconut cream, sauce, juice and sugar; bring to the boil. Simmer, uncovered, 20 minutes. Add meatballs to pan with peas; simmer, uncovered, until meatballs are cooked through and peas are tender.
4  Serve bowls of curry sprinkled with sprouts, coriander leaves, nuts and chilli.

prep + cook time 1 hour  serves 4
nutritional count per serving  80.5g total fat (44.7g saturated fat); 4243kJ (1015 cal); 19.7g carbohydrate; 50.6g protein; 9.1g fibre

# harissa braised vegetables with orange and mint couscous

2 medium carrots (240g)
2 medium zucchini (240g)
2 small leeks (400g)
1 teaspoon olive oil
1 medium brown onion (150g), chopped finely
1 clove garlic, crushed
1 stalk celery (150g), trimmed, chopped coarsely
3 teaspoons harissa paste
1 tablespoon tomato paste
400g (12½ ounces) canned crushed tomatoes
1¼ cups (310ml) water
1 tablespoon orange juice
¼ cup (20g) roasted flaked almonds

ORANGE AND MINT COUSCOUS
1½ cups (300g) couscous
1 teaspoon olive oil
1½ cups (375ml) boiling water
2 teaspoons finely grated orange rind
1 tablespoon orange juice
2 tablespoons coarsely chopped fresh mint

1  Preheat oven to 180°C/350°F.
2  Quarter carrots and zucchini lengthways; cut into 4cm (1½ inch) lengths. Halve leeks lengthways; cut into 6cm (2½ inch) lengths.
3  Heat oil in medium flameproof dish; cook onion and garlic, stirring, until onion softens. Add carrot, zucchini, leek, celery, harissa paste, tomato paste, undrained tomatoes and the water; bring to the boil.
4  Cover dish, transfer to oven; cook about 40 minutes or until vegetables are tender. Stir in juice.
5  Meanwhile, make orange and mint couscous.
6  Divide couscous and braised vegetables among serving bowls; top with nuts.

**orange and mint couscous**  Combine couscous, oil and the water in medium heatproof bowl. Cover; stand about 5 minutes or until liquid is absorbed, fluffing with fork occasionally. Stir in remaining ingredients.

**prep + cook time** 1 hour 10 minutes  **serves** 4
**nutritional count per serving** 7.6g total fat (0.8g saturated fat); 1743kJ (417 cal); 71.1g carbohydrate; 15.1g protein; 8.6g fibre

**note**  Harissa is a Moroccan sauce or paste made from dried chillies, cumin, garlic, oil and caraway seeds. The paste, available in a tube, is very hot and should not be used in large amounts; bottled harissa sauce, while still hot, is milder. It is available from supermarkets and Middle-Eastern grocery stores.

# chicken, chilli and tomato stew

2 tablespoons olive oil
1kg (2 pounds) chicken thigh fillets,
  chopped coarsely
1 medium brown onion (150g), chopped finely
3 cloves garlic, crushed
½ teaspoon ground cumin
800g (1½ pounds) canned chopped tomatoes
1 cup (250ml) chicken stock
1 tablespoon coarsely chopped fresh oregano
¼ cup (60g) drained sliced jalapeño chillies
400g (12½ ounces) canned kidney beans,
  rinsed, drained

1  Heat half the oil in large deep frying pan; cook chicken, in batches, until browned. Remove from pan.
2  Heat remaining oil in same pan; cook onion and garlic, stirring, until onion softens. Add cumin; cook, stirring, until fragrant.
3  Return chicken to pan with undrained tomatoes and stock; bring to the boil. Simmer, covered, about 25 minutes or until sauce thickens slightly.
4  Add oregano, chillies and beans; stir until mixture is heated through.

**prep + cook time** 45 minutes  **serves** 4
**nutritional count per serving**  28.3g total fat
(7g saturated fat); 2345kJ (561 cal);
19g carbohydrate; 54.1g protein; 8.1g fibre

# irish lamb and barley stew

2 tablespoons olive oil
1kg (2 pounds) diced lamb shoulder
1 large brown onion (200g), chopped coarsely
2 medium carrots (240g), chopped coarsely
2 stalks celery (300g), trimmed, chopped coarsely
2 cloves garlic, crushed
1 litre (4 cups) chicken stock
2 cups (500ml) water
1 cup (200g) pearl barley
4 sprigs fresh thyme
3 medium potatoes (600g), chopped coarsely
2 cups (160g) finely shredded cabbage
⅓ cup finely chopped fresh flat-leaf parsley

**1** Heat half the oil in large saucepan; cook lamb, in batches, until browned. Remove from pan.
**2** Heat remaining oil in same pan; cook onion, carrot, celery and garlic, stirring, until vegetables soften. Return lamb to pan with stock, the water, barley and thyme; bring to the boil. Simmer, covered, 1 hour, skimming fat from surface occasionally.
**3** Add potato to pan; simmer, uncovered, about 20 minutes or until potato is tender. Add cabbage; simmer, uncovered, until cabbage is just tender. Discard thyme.
**4** Serve stew sprinkled with parsley.

**prep + cook time** 2 hours  **serves** 6
**nutritional count per serving**  22.6g total fat (8.2g saturated fat); 2224kJ (532 cal); 37.4g carbohydrate; 40.4g protein; 8.6g fibre

# lamb korma

⅓ cup (55g) blanched almonds
3 tablespoons ghee
800g (1½ pounds) lamb strips
1 large brown onion (200g), sliced thinly
2 cloves garlic, crushed
4cm (1½ inch) piece fresh ginger (20g), grated
2 teaspoons poppy seeds
½ cup (150g) bottled korma paste
½ cup (125ml) chicken stock
1¼ cups (310ml) pouring cream (see note)
⅓ cup (95g) yogurt

1  Blend or process nuts until finely ground.
2  Heat 2 tablespoons of the ghee in large saucepan; cook lamb, in batches, until browned. Remove from pan.
3  Heat remaining ghee in same pan; cook onion, garlic and ginger, stirring, until onion softens. Add ground nuts, seeds and paste; cook, stirring, until fragrant.
4  Return lamb to pan with stock and cream; simmer, uncovered, about 15 minutes or until sauce thickens slightly.
5  Serve korma with yogurt.

**prep + cook time** 1 hour  **serves** 4
**nutritional count per serving**  84.1g total fat (40.3g saturated fat); 4172kJ (998 cal); 9.2g carbohydrate; 50.6g protein; 6.4g fibre

**note**  It is fine to use just one 300ml carton of cream for this recipe.

# nepalese pork mince curry

2 tablespoons peanut oil
2 tablespoons yellow mustard seeds
2 teaspoons ground cumin
1 teaspoon ground turmeric
2 teaspoons garam masala
3 cloves garlic, crushed
4cm (1½ inch) piece fresh ginger (20g), grated
2 medium brown onions (300g), chopped finely
800g (1½ pounds) minced (ground) pork
½ cup (125ml) water
¼ cup coarsely chopped fresh coriander (cilantro)

1   Heat oil in large frying pan; cook seeds, stirring, about 2 minutes or until seeds pop. Add cumin, turmeric and garam masala; cook, stirring, 2 minutes.
2   Add garlic, ginger and onion to pan; cook, stirring, until onion softens.
3   Add mince to pan; cook, stirring, until cooked through. Add the water; simmer, uncovered, 15 minutes. Remove from heat, stir in coriander.

**prep + cook time** 35 minutes  **serves** 4
**nutritional count per serving**  23.4g total fat (6.9g saturated fat); 1655kJ (396 cal); 4g carbohydrate; 41.4g protein; 2.6g fibre

# thai red chicken curry

2 cups (400g) jasmine rice
2 tablespoons peanut oil
750g (1½ pounds) chicken thigh fillets,
  chopped coarsely
1 large brown onion (200g), chopped coarsely
3 cloves garlic, crushed
2 tablespoons red curry paste
1 fresh long red chilli, halved lengthways,
  sliced thinly
1 teaspoon ground cumin
3 baby eggplants (180g), sliced thickly
1 tablespoon fish sauce
3 fresh kaffir lime leaves, sliced thinly
⅔ cup (160ml) canned coconut milk
¾ cup (180ml) water
150g (4½ ounces) snake beans, cut into 5cm
  (2 inch) lengths
⅓ cup loosely packed fresh coriander
  (cilantro) leaves

1  Cook rice in large saucepan of boiling water,
uncovered, until just tender; drain.
2  Meanwhile, heat half the oil in wok; stir-fry chicken,
in batches, until browned. Remove from wok.
3  Heat remaining oil in wok; stir-fry onion and garlic
until onion softens. Add paste, chilli and cumin;
stir-fry until fragrant. Add eggplant; stir-fry until
browned lightly.
4  Return chicken to wok with sauce, lime leaves,
coconut milk, the water and beans; stir-fry about
5 minutes or until chicken is cooked through and
sauce is thickened slightly.
5  Sprinkle with curry with coriander to serve.

**prep + cook time** 45 minutes  **serves** 4
**nutritional count per serving** 34.4g total fat
(12.6g saturated fat); 3557kJ (851 cal);
86.8g carbohydrate; 46g protein; 6g fibre

**note** You'll need about half a bunch of snake beans
for this recipe. Use green beans, if you prefer.

# spanish chicken casserole

1 tablespoon olive oil
4 chicken drumsticks (600g)
4 chicken thigh cutlets (800g)
1 large brown onion (200g), chopped finely
4 medium potatoes (800g), quartered
½ cup (80g) roasted pine nuts
½ cup (80g) roasted blanched almonds
3 cups (750ml) chicken stock
1 cup (250ml) dry white wine
⅓ cup (80ml) lemon juice
4 cloves garlic, crushed
2 tablespoons fresh thyme leaves
½ cup coarsely chopped fresh flat-leaf parsley
500g (1 pound) baby green beans, trimmed

1  Preheat oven to 180°C/350°F.
2  Heat oil in large flameproof casserole dish; cook chicken, in batches, until browned. Remove from dish.
3  Cook onion in same dish, stirring, until soft. Return chicken to dish with potato, nuts, stock, wine, juice, garlic, thyme and half the parsley; bring to the boil. Cover, transfer to oven; cook in oven about 1 hour or until chicken is cooked through.
4  Meanwhile, boil, steam or microwave beans until tender; drain.
5  Serve chicken with beans; sprinkle with remaining parsley.

**prep + cook time** 1 hour 35 minutes  **serves** 4
**nutritional count per serving** 61.4g total fat (12.4g saturated fat); 4050kJ (969 cal); 35g carbohydrate; 57g protein; 10.4g fibre

# cauliflower, pea and paneer balti

1 tablespoon sesame seeds
2 tablespoons vegetable oil
6 dried curry leaves
¼ teaspoon black mustard seeds
1 teaspoon ground coriander
1 teaspoon hot chilli powder
1 teaspoon ground cumin
2 cloves garlic, crushed
400g (12½ ounces) canned diced tomatoes
1kg (2 pounds) cauliflower, trimmed, cut into florets
½ cup (125ml) water
1 cup (120g) frozen peas
400g (12½ ounces) paneer cheese, cut into
  2.5cm (1 inch) cubes
¼ cup coarsely chopped fresh coriander (cilantro)

1  Heat wok; roast sesame seeds until browned
lightly. Remove from wok.
2  Heat oil in wok; stir-fry curry leaves and mustard
seeds until seeds pop.
3  Add ground coriander, chilli, cumin and garlic to
wok; stir-fry until fragrant. Add undrained tomatoes;
simmer, stirring, about 2 minutes or until mixture
thickens slightly.
4  Add cauliflower and the water; stir-fry until
cauliflower is almost tender. Add peas, cheese
and chopped coriander; stir-fry until hot. Remove
from heat; sprinkle with sesame seeds.

**prep + cook time** 45 minutes  **serves** 4
**nutritional count per serving**  34.9g total fat
(16.7g saturated fat); 2002kJ (479 cal);
11.4g carbohydrate; 26.6g protein; 8.1g fibre

**note**  Haloumi cheese is a good substitute if
paneer is not available.

# beef and horseradish stew with kumara mash

2 tablespoons olive oil
1.5kg (3 pounds) beef chuck steak, cut into
  5cm (2 inch) cubes
3 medium brown onions (450g), sliced into wedges
3 cloves garlic, crushed
8cm (3 inch) piece fresh ginger (40g), grated
2 teaspoons curry powder
¼ cup (35g) plain (all-purpose) flour
3 cups (750ml) beef stock
1 tablespoon worcestershire sauce
2 tablespoons horseradish cream
¼ cup coarsely chopped fresh flat-leaf parsley

KUMARA MASH
1kg (2 pounds) kumara (orange sweet potato),
  chopped coarsely
500g (1 pound) potatoes, chopped coarsely
¾ cup (180ml) pouring cream, warmed
60g (2 ounces) butter

1  Preheat oven to 120°C/250°F.
2  Heat oil in large flameproof casserole dish; cook
beef, in batches, until browned. Remove from dish.
Cook onion, garlic and ginger in dish, stirring, until
onion softens. Add curry powder and flour; cook,
stirring, 5 minutes.
3  Return beef to dish with stock and sauce; stir
over heat until mixture boils and thickens. Cover
dish tightly; cook for 3 hours, stirring occasionally.
4  Meanwhile, make kumara potato mash.
5  Remove beef mixture from heat; stir through
horseradish cream and parsley; serve with mash.
kumara potato mash  Boil, steam or microwave
kumara and potato, separately, until tender; drain.
Mash kumara and potato with warmed cream and
butter until smooth; cover to keep warm.

prep + cook time 4 hours  serves 6
nutritional count per serving  39.9g total fat
(20.2g saturated fat); 3177kJ (760 cal);
41.5g carbohydrate; 59.1g protein; 5.6g fibre

note  Recipe can be made ahead to the end of step 3;
cool then cover and refrigerate overnight or freeze.

# beef stew with parsley dumplings

1kg (2 pounds) beef chuck steak, cut into
  5cm (2 inch) pieces
2 tablespoons plain (all-purpose) flour
2 tablespoons olive oil
30g (1 ounce) butter
2 medium brown onions (300g), chopped coarsely
2 cloves garlic, crushed
2 medium carrots (240g), chopped coarsely
1 cup (250ml) dry red wine
2 tablespoons tomato paste
2 cups (500ml) beef stock
4 sprigs fresh thyme

PARSLEY DUMPLINGS
1 cup (150g) self-raising flour
60g (2 ounces) butter
1 egg, beaten lightly
¼ cup (20g) coarsely grated parmesan cheese
¼ cup finely chopped fresh flat-leaf parsley
⅓ cup (50g) drained sun-dried tomatoes in oil,
  finely chopped
¼ cup (60ml) milk, approximately

1  Preheat oven to 180°C/350°F.
2  Coat beef in flour; shake off excess. Heat oil in large flameproof dish; cook beef, in batches, on stove top, until browned. Remove from dish.
3  Melt butter in same dish; cook onion, garlic and carrot, stirring, until vegetables soften. Add wine; cook, stirring, until liquid reduces to ¼ cup. Return beef with paste, stock and thyme; bring to the boil.
4  Cover dish, transfer to oven; cook 1¾ hours.
5  Meanwhile, make parsley dumpling mixture.
6  Remove dish from oven. Drop level tablespoons of dumpling mixture, about 2cm (¾ inch) apart, onto top of stew. Cook, uncovered, about 20 minutes or until dumplings are browned lightly and cooked.

parsley dumplings  Place flour in medium bowl; rub in butter. Stir in egg, cheese, parsley, tomato and enough milk to make a soft, sticky dough.

prep + cook time 3 hours  serves 4
nutritional count per serving  39.7g total fat (17.4g saturated fat); 3457kJ (827 cal); 43g carbohydrate; 63.9g protein; 6.7g fibre

# lemon grass chicken curry

1 tablespoon vegetable oil
24 chicken drumettes (1.7kg)
1 medium brown onion (150g), sliced thinly
3 cloves garlic, crushed
½ teaspoon cracked black pepper
3 x 10cm (4 inch) sticks (60g) fresh lemon grass,
  chopped finely
1 fresh long green chilli, chopped finely
¼ cup (75g) mild curry paste
1 tablespoon grated palm sugar
½ cup (125ml) chicken stock
½ cup (125ml) water
1 medium red capsicum (bell pepper) (200g),
  sliced thinly
1 medium carrot (120g), cut into matchsticks
4 green onions (scallions), sliced thinly

1  Heat oil in large flameproof casserole dish; cook chicken, in batches, until browned. Remove from dish. Drain and discard cooking juices.
2  Cook brown onion, garlic, pepper, lemon grass and chilli in same dish, stirring, until onion softens. Add paste; cook, stirring, until fragrant. Return chicken to dish; cook, stirring, 5 minutes.
3  Add sugar, stock and the water; cook, covered, 10 minutes. Uncover; simmer about 10 minutes or until chicken is cooked through. Remove chicken from dish; cover to keep warm.
4  Add capsicum and carrot to dish; cook, uncovered, about 5 minutes or until curry sauce thickens and vegetables are just tender. Stir green onion into curry off the heat.
5  Serve chicken topped with vegetable mixture.

**prep + cook time** 1 hour 10 minutes  **serves** 4
**nutritional count per serving**  36.3g total fat
(9g saturated fat); 2286kJ (547 cal);
9.9g carbohydrate; 43.8g protein; 4.3g fibre

# pork cabbage rolls

18 large cabbage leaves
½ cup (100g) uncooked white long-grain rice
250g (8 ounces) minced (ground) pork
1 medium brown onion (150g), chopped finely
¼ cup finely chopped fresh dill
1 clove garlic, crushed
1 tablespoon tomato paste
2 teaspoons ground cumin
1 teaspoon ground coriander
1 teaspoon ground allspice
4 cloves garlic, quartered
2 medium tomatoes (300g), chopped coarsely
800g (1½ pounds) canned crushed tomatoes
¼ cup (60ml) lemon juice

1 Discard thick stems from 15 cabbage leaves; reserve remaining leaves. Boil, steam or microwave trimmed leaves until just pliable; drain. Rinse under cold water; drain. Pat dry with absorbent paper.
2 Combine rice, pork, onion, dill, crushed garlic, paste and spices in medium bowl.
3 Place one trimmed leaf, vein-side up, on board; cut leaf in half lengthways. Place 1 rounded teaspoon of the pork mixture at stem end of each half; roll each half firmly to enclose filling. Repeat with remaining trimmed leaves.
4 Place reserved leaves in base of large saucepan. Place only enough rolls, seam-side down, in single layer, to completely cover leaves in base of pan. Top with quartered garlic, chopped fresh tomato then remaining rolls.
5 Pour undrained tomatoes and juice over cabbage rolls; bring to the boil. Simmer, covered, 1 hour. Uncover; simmer about 30 minutes or until cabbage rolls are cooked through.

**prep + cook time** 2 hours 40 minutes  **serves** 6
**nutritional count per serving**  3.6g total fat (1.1g saturated fat); 803kJ (192 cal); 24.7g carbohydrate; 14.3g protein; 9.7g fibre

**Serve with** thick greek-style yogurt flavoured with a little finely chopped preserved lemon.

# puddings & desserts

## crêpes suzette

¾ cup (110g) plain (all-purpose) flour
3 eggs
2 tablespoons vegetable oil
¾ cup (180ml) milk

ORANGE SAUCE
125g (4 ounces) unsalted butter
½ cup (110g) caster (superfine) sugar
1½ cups (375ml) orange juice
2 tablespoons lemon juice
⅓ cup (80ml) orange-flavoured liqueur

1   Sift flour into medium bowl, make well in centre; add eggs and oil then gradually whisk in milk until smooth. Pour batter into large jug, cover; stand 1 hour.
2   Heat greased heavy-based crêpe pan or small frying pan; pour ¼ cup of batter into pan, tilting pan to coat base. Cook, over low heat, until browned lightly, loosening edge of crêpe with a spatula. Turn crêpe; brown other side. Remove crêpe from pan; cover to keep warm. Repeat with remaining batter to make a total of 8 crêpes, greasing pan each time.

3   Make orange sauce. Fold crêpes in half then in half again, place in sauce; warm over low heat.
4   Remove crêpes to serving plates; pour hot sauce over crêpes. Serve with orange segments.

orange sauce  Melt butter in large frying pan, add sugar; cook, stirring, until mixture begins to brown. Add strained juices; bring to the boil. Reduce heat; simmer, uncovered, about 3 minutes or until a golden colour. Remove from heat; add liqueur, ignite.

prep + cook time 1 hour 40 minutes (+ standing)
serves 4
nutritional count per serving 41g total fat (20.5g saturated fat); 3039kJ (727 cal); 66.9g carbohydrate; 10.3g protein; 1.3g fibre

note  Make sure overhead exhaust fans are turned off before igniting the orange sauce. Be very careful when igniting the sauce – use extra long matches, available from supermarkets or camping stores. Igniting the sauce burns off the alcohol, leaving a more intense flavour. If you prefer, the sauce can be served as is, without first igniting it.

# bread and butter pudding

6 slices white bread (270g)
30g (1 ounce) butter, softened
½ cup (80g) sultanas
¼ teaspoon ground nutmeg

CUSTARD
1½ cups (375ml) milk
2 cups (500ml) pouring cream
⅓ cup (75g) caster (superfine) sugar
1 teaspoon vanilla extract
4 eggs

1  Preheat oven to 150°C/300°F. Grease shallow
2-litre (8-cup) ovenproof dish.
2  Make custard.
3  Trim crusts from bread. Spread each slice
with butter; cut into four triangles. Layer bread,
overlapping, in dish; sprinkle with sultanas.
Pour custard over bread; sprinkle with nutmeg.
4  Place ovenproof dish in large baking dish; add
enough boiling water to come halfway up side of
ovenproof dish. Bake about 45 minutes or until
pudding is set. Remove pudding from baking dish;
stand 5 minutes before serving.
5  Dust with sifted icing (confectioners') sugar to
serve, if you like.

custard  Combine milk, cream, sugar and extract in
medium saucepan; bring to the boil. Whisk eggs in
large bowl; whisking constantly, gradually add hot
milk mixture to egg mixture.

prep + cook time 1 hour 15 minutes  serves 6
nutritional count per serving  48.6g total fat
(30.4g saturated fat); 2859kJ (684 cal);
49.3g carbohydrate; 12.4g protein; 1.8g fibre

# caramelised apple tea cakes

125g (4 ounces) butter, softened
1 teaspoon vanilla extract
⅔ cup (150g) caster (superfine) sugar
2 eggs
1¼ cups (185g) self-raising flour
½ cup (75g) plain (all-purpose) flour
1 teaspoon mixed spice
½ teaspoon ground cinnamon
1 cup (250ml) buttermilk
1 large apple (200g), peeled, grated coarsely

CARAMELISED APPLES
2 small apples (260g)
75g (2½ ounces) butter
⅓ cup (75g) firmly packed light brown sugar

1   Make caramelised apples.
2   Preheat oven to 180°C/350°F. Grease two
six-hole (¾-cup/180ml) texas muffin pans.
3   Place one slice caramelised apple in each pan
hole; spoon caramel sauce over apple.
4   Beat butter, extract and sugar in small bowl with
electric mixer until light and fluffy. Beat in eggs,
one at a time. Transfer mixture to large bowl; stir
in sifted dry ingredients and buttermilk, in two
batches. Stir in apple. Divide mixture among pan
holes; bake about 30 minutes.
5   Stand cakes in pan 5 minutes before turning,
top-side up, onto wire rack. Serve cakes warm.

caramelised apples  Slice each unpeeled apple
into six 1cm (½ inch) thick slices. Stir butter and
sugar in large frying pan over low heat until sugar
dissolves. Add apple slices to caramel sauce; cook,
turning occasionally, about 3 minutes or until
browned lightly.

prep + cook time 1 hour  makes 12
nutritional count per cake 10.1g total fat
(6.2g saturated fat); 974kJ (233 cal);
30.5g carbohydrate; 4.3g protein; 1.1g fibre

# lemon curd, blueberry and meringue trifle

2 cups (500ml) grape juice
85g (3 ounce) packet blueberry jelly (jello) crystals
200g (6½ ounce) store-bought sponge cake,
  cut into 2.5cm (1 inch) pieces
¼ cup (60ml) sweet sherry
2 teaspoons finely grated lemon rind
¾ cup (180ml) lemon juice
1 cup (220g) caster (superfine) sugar
4 eggs
80g (2½ ounces) butter, chopped coarsely
1 teaspoon gelatine
1 tablespoon water
1¼ cups (310ml) thickened (heavy) cream (see note)
50g (1½ ounces) meringue, chopped coarsely
2 cups (300g) fresh blueberries

1  Bring grape juice to the boil in small saucepan; stir in jelly crystals until dissolved. Pour mixture into shallow container. Refrigerate about 20 minutes or until jelly is almost set.
2  Place cake in 3-litre (12-cup) bowl; sprinkle with sherry.
3  Combine rind, juice, sugar, eggs and butter in medium heatproof bowl. Place over medium saucepan of simmering water; cook, stirring, about 15 minutes or until curd coats the back of a spoon.
4  Sprinkle gelatine over the water in small heatproof jug. Stand jug in small saucepan of simmering water; stir until gelatine dissolves. Stir gelatine mixture into warm lemon curd. Cool to room temperature.
5  Pour jelly over cake; refrigerate 15 minutes. Top with lemon curd. Cover; refrigerate 3 hours or overnight.
6  Just before serving, beat cream in small bowl with electric mixer until soft peaks form; spread over curd. Sprinkle with meringue and berries.

**prep + cook time** 50 minutes
(+ refrigeration and cooling) **serves** 6
**nutritional count per serving** 34.7g total fat
(21g saturated fat); 3168kJ (758 cal);
97.5g carbohydrate; 10.6g protein; 1.3g fibre

**note** It is fine to use just one 300ml carton of cream for this recipe.

# berry, almond and coconut slice

2 cups (300g) frozen mixed berries
1 cup (220g) caster (superfine) sugar
1 tablespoon lime juice
90g (3 ounces) butter, softened
1 egg
⅔ cup (100g) plain (all-purpose) flour
¼ cup (35g) self-raising flour
1 tablespoon custard powder

ALMOND COCONUT TOPPING
2 eggs, beaten lightly
1½ cups (75g) flaked coconut
1 cup (80g) flaked almonds
¼ cup (55g) caster (superfine) sugar

1  Preheat oven to 180°C/350°F. Grease 20cm x
30cm (8 inch x 12 inch) lamington pan; line base
with baking paper (parchment), extending paper
5cm (2 inches) over long sides.
2  Combine half the berries, half the sugar and
the juice in small saucepan; stir over low heat until
sugar dissolves. Bring to the boil, then simmer,
uncovered, stirring occasionally, about 20 minutes
or until mixture thickens; cool 10 minutes. Stir in
remaining berries.
3  Beat butter, egg and remaining sugar in small
bowl with electric mixer until light and fluffy; stir in
sifted flours and custard powder. Spread dough
into pan; spread with berry mixture.
4  Make almond coconut topping; sprinkle topping
over berry mixture. Bake about 40 minutes; cool,
then cut into 16 slices.

**almond coconut topping** Combine ingredients in
small bowl.

**prep + cook time** 1 hour 25 minutes (+ cooling)
**serves** 16
**nutritional count per serving** 11.6g total fat
(6.2g saturated fat); 932kJ (223 cal);
25g carbohydrate; 3.8g protein; 1.9g fibre

# choc-cherry microwave self-saucing pudding

60g (2 ounces) butter, chopped
1½ cups (225g) self-raising flour
1 cup (220g) caster (superfine) sugar
⅓ cup (35g) cocoa powder
1¼ cups (310ml) milk
1 teaspoon vanilla extract
2 x 55g (2 ounce) Cherry Ripe bars,
  chopped coarsely
½ cup (110g) firmly packed light brown sugar
1 tablespoon cocoa powder, extra
2 cups (500ml) boiling water
50g (1½ ounces) butter, chopped, extra

1  Melt butter in deep 3-litre (12-cup) microwave-safe dish, uncovered, on HIGH (100%) in microwave oven about 1 minute or until butter has melted.
2  Add sifted flour, caster sugar and cocoa to dish with milk and extract; whisk until smooth. Stir in Cherry Ripe.
3  Combine brown sugar and sifted extra cocoa in medium jug; gradually stir in the boiling water. Add extra butter; stir until butter melts. Carefully pour syrup mixture evenly over pudding mixture.
4  Cook, uncovered, on HIGH (100%) in microwave oven about 15 minutes or until just cooked in centre. Stand 5 minutes before serving with ice-cream or cream, if you like.

prep + cook time 25 minutes  serves 8
nutritional count per serving  16.9g total fat
(11.3g saturated fat); 1884kJ (450 cal);
71.1g carbohydrate; 5.8g protein; 2g fibre

# honey spice sponge cake

2 eggs
½ cup (110g) caster (superfine) sugar
⅓ cup (50g) wheaten cornflour (cornstarch)
1½ tablespoons custard powder
1 teaspoon mixed spice
½ teaspoon cream of tartar
¼ teaspoon bicarbonate of soda (baking soda)
1¼ cups (310ml) thickened (heavy) cream (see note)
2 tablespoons honey
1 tablespoon icing (confectioners') sugar

1 Preheat oven to 180°C/350°F. Grease 25cm x 30cm (10 inch x 12 inch) swiss roll pan; line base with baking paper (parchment), extending paper 5cm (2 inches) over long sides.
2 Beat eggs and ⅓ cup of the sugar in small bowl with electric mixer about 10 minutes or until thick and creamy.
3 Meanwhile, triple-sift cornflour, custard powder, spice, cream of tartar and soda onto baking paper. Sift flour mixture over egg mixture; fold ingredients together. Spread mixture into pan; bake 10 minutes.
4 Place a piece of baking paper cut the same size as the pan on bench; sprinkle evenly with remaining sugar. Turn cake onto sugared paper; peel lining paper away. Cool.
5 Beat cream and honey in small bowl with electric mixer until firm peaks form.
6 Cut edges from all sides of sponge then cut widthways into three rectangles. Place one piece of sponge on plate; spread with half the cream mixture. Top with second piece of sponge and remaining cream. Finish with remaining sponge and dust with sifted icing sugar.

**prep + cook time** 25 minutes  **serves** 6
**nutritional count per serving** 20.1g total fat (12.6g saturated fat); 1480kJ (354 cal); 39.9g carbohydrate; 3.7g protein; 0.1g fibre

**note** It is fine to use just one 300ml carton of cream for this recipe.

# lemon meringue pudding

200g (6½ ounces) store-bought sponge cake
1¾ cups (430ml) pouring cream
1 teaspoon vanilla extract
1 teaspoon finely grated lemon rind
⅓ cup (80ml) lemon juice
6 eggs
¾ cup (165g) caster (superfine) sugar
280g (9 ounces) bottled lemon butter

MERINGUE TOPPING
3 egg whites
¾ cup (165g) caster (superfine) sugar
1 tablespoon caster (superfine) sugar, extra
yellow food colouring

1  Preheat oven to 170°C/325°F. Lightly grease round 2-litre (8-cup) ovenproof dish.
2  Cut sponge cake into 2.5cm (1 inch) pieces; place pieces randomly in prepared dish.
3  Combine cream, extract, rind and juice in small saucepan over low heat; stir until hot.
4  Whisk eggs and sugar in large bowl until combined. Whisking constantly, pour hot cream mixture into egg mixture; pour into dish over sponge cake. Bake, uncovered, about 45 minutes. Remove pudding from oven; increase oven temperature to 180°C/350°F. Cool pudding 10 minutes.
5  Meanwhile, make meringue topping.
6  Using rubber spatula, carefully spread lemon butter over surface of pudding. Spoon meringue topping over pudding to completely cover surface; sprinkle yellow sugar evenly over meringue. Bake, uncovered, about 15 minutes or until meringue is browned lightly. Serve hot with cream or ice-cream.

**meringue topping**  Beat egg whites in small bowl with electric mixer until soft peaks form; add sugar, a tablespoon at a time, beating until sugar dissolves between additions. Tint extra sugar with a little yellow colouring in small bowl.

**prep + cook time** 1 hour 30 minutes  **serves** 8
**nutritional count per serving**  27.4g total fat (17.5g saturated fat); 2579kJ (617 cal); 80.7g carbohydrate; 9.7g protein; 0.4g fibre

## plum clafoutis

Preheat oven to 200°C/400°F. Grease shallow 2.5-litre (10-cup) ovenproof dish. Place 10 halved, seeded small plums in medium baking dish with 1 halved cinnamon stick and ¼ cup water; sprinkle with ¼ cup light brown sugar. Cook about 15 minutes or until plums soften. Remove cinnamon from dish and add to medium saucepan with ⅔ cup each milk and pouring cream, and 1 teaspoon vanilla extract; bring to the boil. Cool; remove cinnamon stick. Whisk 4 eggs and ½ cup caster (superfine) sugar in medium bowl until light and frothy; whisk in ¼ cup plain (all-purpose) flour. Whisk flour mixture into cream mixture. Place drained plums in dish; pour cream mixture over plums. Bake about 30 minutes or until browned lightly. Dust with icing (confectioners') sugar.

**prep + cook time** 1 hour 10 minutes **serves** 6
**nutritional count per serving** 16.1g total fat
(9.3g saturated fat); 1417kJ (339 cal);
46.2g carbohydrate; 7.1g protein; 2.4g fibre

## banana split

Preheat grill (broiler). Halve 4 bananas lengthways. Place bananas, cut-sides up, on oven tray; sprinkle with 2 tablespoons light brown sugar. Grill about 3 minutes or until sugar melts. Meanwhile, melt 100g (3 ounces) dark eating (semi-sweet) chocolate with 2 tablespoons thickened (heavy) cream in small bowl set over small saucepan of simmering water. Beat 1 cup thickened (heavy) cream with 1 tablespoon dark rum in small bowl with electric mixer until soft peaks form. Place 2 banana halves in each of four dishes; top each with a scoop of chocolate and vanilla ice-cream. Top each with whipped cream; drizzle with chocolate then sprinkle evenly with ⅔ cup coarsely chopped roasted pecans and ⅓ cup toasted shredded coconut.

**prep + cook time** 30 minutes **serves** 4
**nutritional count per serving** 60.1g total fat
(31.7g saturated fat); 3618kJ (865 cal);
65.7g carbohydrate; 9.9g protein; 5.8g fibre

## ginger sticky date pudding

Preheat oven to 200°C/400°F. Grease deep 20cm (8 inch) round cake pan; line base with baking paper (parchment). Combine 1 cup seeded dried dates, ¼ cup glacé ginger, 1 teaspoon bicarbonate of soda (baking soda) and 1 cup boiling water in food processor; stand 5 minutes then add 50g (1½ ounces) butter and ½ cup firmly packed light brown sugar. Process until mixture is almost smooth. Add 2 eggs, 1 cup self-raising flour and 1 teaspoon ground ginger; process until combined. Pour mixture into pan; bake about 45 minutes. Stand 10 minutes before turning onto serving plate. Meanwhile, stir 1¼ cups (310ml) pouring cream, ¾ cup firmly packed light brown sugar and 75g (2½ ounces) chopped butter in medium saucepan over low heat until sauce is smooth. Serve pudding warm with sauce.

**prep + cook time** 55 minutes  **serves** 8
**nutritional count per serving** 30.1g total fat (19.6g saturated fat); 2337kJ (559 cal); 65.1g carbohydrate; 4.7g protein; 2.4g fibre

**note** It is fine to use just one 300ml carton of cream for this recipe.

## rice pudding with cardamom and raisins

Combine 1 litre (4 cups) milk, 1¼ cups (310ml) pouring cream, 1 cup arborio rice, and ½ cup caster (superfine) sugar in large saucepan; stir over heat, without boiling, until sugar dissolves. Bring to the boil; reduce heat. Cook, stirring, about 20 minutes or until rice is tender. Meanwhile, melt 40g (1½ ounces) butter in small saucepan; stir in ¼ cup firmly packed light brown sugar and 2 peeled, cored and quartered medium apples. Stir over low heat about 10 minutes or until sauce is thickened and apples are tender. Stir in ½ teaspoon each ground cardamom and cinnamon and ¾ cup raisins; cook, stirring, 5 minutes. Serve rice pudding topped with apples.

**prep + cook time** 30 minutes  **serves** 4
**nutritional count per serving** 51g total fat (33.4g saturated fat); 4193kJ (1003 cal); 120g carbohydrate; 14.1g protein; 2.7g fibre

**note** It is fine to use just one 300ml carton of cream for this recipe.

## peach and walnut galettes

Preheat oven to 180°C/350°F. Grease oven tray; line with baking paper (parchment). Cut 1 sheet ready-rolled puff pastry into quarters, place quarters on tray; prick with fork, brush with 20g melted butter. Divide ¼ cup raw sugar and ⅓ cup finely chopped walnuts among pastry squares, leaving 1cm (½ inch) border around each. Slice canned peach halves thinly; divide among pastry squares. Bake about 10 minutes or until pastry is golden brown.

**prep + cook time** 15 minutes **makes** 4
**nutritional count per galette** 20.5g total fat (8.2g saturated fat); 1451kJ (347 cal); 35.9g carbohydrate; 4.1g protein; 2g fibre

## rhubarb and coconut cake

Preheat oven to 140°C/275°F. Grease 14cm x 21cm (5½ inch x 8½ inch) loaf pan; line base with baking paper (parchment). Combine 1½ cups self-raising flour, 1¼ cups caster (superfine) sugar and 1¼ cups desiccated coconut in medium bowl; stir in 125g (4 ounces) melted butter, 3 lightly beaten eggs, ½ cup milk and ½ teaspoon vanilla extract until combined. Spread half of the cake mixture into prepared pan; sprinkle evenly with 1 cup finely chopped rhubarb, spread remaining cake mixture over rhubarb. Cut 5 trimmed rhubarb stalks into 12cm (5 inch) lengths. Arrange rhubarb pieces over top of cake; sprinkle with 2 tablespoons demerara sugar. Bake, uncovered, about 1½ hours. Stand cake in pan 5 minutes before turning, top-side up, onto wire rack to cool.

**prep + cook time** 1 hour 55 minutes **serves** 8
**nutritional count per serving** 24.8g total fat (17.4g saturated fat); 2044kJ (489 cal); 61g carbohydrate; 7.5g protein; 4.7g fibre

## warm chocolate pavlovas

Preheat oven to 180°C/350°F. Line large oven tray with baking paper (parchment). Beat 2 egg whites, 1⅓ cups icing (confectioners') sugar and ⅓ cup boiling water in small bowl with electric mixer about 10 minutes or until firm peaks form. Fold 1 tablespoon sifted cocoa powder into meringue. Drop six equal amounts of mixture onto tray; use the back of a spoon to create well in centre of mounds. Bake about 25 minutes or until firm to touch. Meanwhile, blend 1 tablespoon each cornflour (cornstarch), cocoa powder and caster (superfine) sugar with 1 cup milk in small saucepan. Stir in 2 egg yolks. Stir over heat until sauce boils and thickens. Serve pavlovas straight from the oven, topped with sauce and scoops of chocolate ice-cream.

**prep + cook time** 40 minutes  **serves** 4
**nutritional count per serving**  14.5g total fat (9g saturated fat); 2011kJ (481 cal); 79.5g carbohydrate; 7.4g protein; 0.2g fibre

## apple and blackberry jellies

Prepare a 85g (3 ounce) packet blackcurrant jelly (jello) crystals according to packet instructions. Divide 1 cup frozen blackberries and 1 peeled, cored and finely chopped medium apple among four ¾-cup (180ml) glasses, pour jelly over the top. Refrigerate about 3 hours or until jelly has set. Beat ½ cup thickened (heavy) cream and 1 tablespoon icing (confectioners') sugar in small bowl with electric mixer until soft peaks form. Serve jellies topped with whipped cream.

**prep + cook time** 10 minutes (+ refrigeration)
**serves** 4
**nutritional count per serving**  11.6g total fat (7.6g saturated fat); 986kJ (239 cal); 30.1g carbohydrate; 2.9g protein; 1.4g fibre

# glossary

**ANTIPASTO, CHAR-GRILLED** marinated char-grilled vegetables, such as capsicum, eggplant, zucchini, artichoke, etc. Available from delicatessens or supermarkets.

**ARTICHOKES, MARINATED** the tender centre (heart) of the globe artichoke purchased canned or in glass jars in brine or oil.

**ASIAN GREENS, BABY** a packaged mix of baby buk choy, choy sum, gai lan and water spinach. Available from selected supermarkets.

**BALSAMIC GLAZE** a rich, dark brown glaze made from concentrated balsamic vinegar and brown sugar; available from major supermarkets.

**BASIL** an aromatic herb; there are many types, but the most commonly used is sweet, or common, basil.
**thai** also known as horapa; has smallish leaves and a sweet licorice/aniseed taste. Available in Asian supermarkets and greengrocers.

**BEANS**
**borlotti** also known as roman or pink beans. Interchangeable with pinto beans because of the similarity in appearance – both are pale pink or beige with dark red streaks.
**broad** also known as fava or windsor beans; available dried, fresh, canned and frozen. Fresh and frozen forms should be peeled twice, discarding both the outer long green pod and the beige-green tough inner shell.
**four bean mix** made up of kidney beans, butter beans, chickpeas and cannellini beans.
**sprouts** also known as bean shoots; tender new growths of assorted beans and seeds germinated for consumption as sprouts. The most readily available are mung bean, soy bean, alfalfa and snow pea sprouts.

**BEEF**
**eye-fillet** tenderloin fillet; has a fine texture and is extremely tender. Is more expensive than other cuts.
**rump** a tender, boneless cut taken from the upper hindquarter.
**scotch fillet** cut from the muscle running along the spine.

**BEETROOT** also known as red beets or beets; firm, round root vegetable.

**BISCUITS**
**scotch finger** made from flour, sugar, butter, egg and condensed milk; can be broken into two finger-sized pieces.
**sponge finger** also known as savoy biscuits, savoiardi or lady's fingers; these Italian-style crisp fingers are made from sponge-cake mixture.

**BREAD**
**brioche** rich, yeast-risen French bread made with butter and eggs. Available from pâtisseries and better bakeries.
**ciabatta** in Italian it means 'slipper,' which is the traditional shape of this popular white bread with a crisp crust.
**tortillas** thin, round unleavened bread originating in Mexico; two kinds are available, one made from wheat flour and the other from corn (maize meal).

**BREADCRUMBS, STALE** one- or two-day-old bread made into crumbs by blending or processing.

**BUTTER** use salted or unsalted butter; 125g is equal to one stick (4 ounces).

**BUTTERMILK** originally the term given to the slightly sour liquid left after butter was churned from cream, today it is made similarly to yogurt. Sold alongside all fresh milk products in supermarkets; despite the implication of its name, it's low in fat.

**CAJUN SPICE MIX** a blend of herbs and spices including basil, paprika, tarragon, onion, fennel, thyme and cayenne; available at spice shops and most supermarkets.

**CAPERS** the grey-green buds of a warm climate shrub, sold either dried and salted or pickled in a vinegar brine.
**baby capers**, those picked early, are very small, fuller-flavoured and more expensive than the full-sized ones. Capers, whether packed in brine or in salt, must be rinsed well before using.

**CHEESE**
**bocconcini** walnut-sized, fresh, baby mozzarella, a delicate, semi-soft, white cheese. Spoils rapidly, so must be kept under refrigeration, in brine, for one or two days at most.

**cheddar** this semi-hard cows'-milk cheese is eaten throughout the world.
**fetta** a crumbly goat- or sheep-milk cheese with a sharp salty taste.
**goat's** made from goats' milk; has an earthy, strong taste. Comes in soft and firm textures and in various shapes and sizes; may be rolled in ash or herbs.
**mascarpone** fresh, unripened, smooth, triple cream cheese with a rich, sweet, slightly acidic, taste.
**parmesan** also known as parmigiana; a hard, grainy cows'-milk cheese.
**ricotta** a sweet, moist, low-fat, fresh unripened cheese made from whey.

**CHERVIL** also known as cicily; a curly-leafed herb with a mild fennel flavour.

**CHICKEN**
**tenderloin** thin strip of meat lying just under the breast.
**thigh fillet** thigh with the skin and centre bone removed.

**CHILLI** available in many different types and sizes. Use rubber gloves when seeding and chopping fresh chillies as they can burn your skin. Removing seeds and membranes lessens the heat level.
**flakes** deep-red, dehydrated chilli slices and whole seeds.
**jam** a sweet, sourish tangy jam sold in jars at supermarkets or Asian food stores. Used in sauces, stir-fries and some soups. After opening, store in the refrigerator.
**long red** available fresh and dried; a generic term used for any moderately hot, long (6cm-8cm), thin chilli.
**red thai** small, medium hot and bright red in colour.

**CHOCOLATE, DARK EATING** also known as semi-sweet or luxury chocolate; made of a high percentage of cocoa liquor and cocoa butter, and a little added sugar.

**CHORIZO** a sausage of Spanish origin. Is made of coarsely ground pork and is highly seasoned with garlic and chillies.

**CINNAMON** dried inner bark of the shoots of the cinnamon tree; available in stick (quill) or ground form.

**CONSOMMÉ** a clear soup usually of beef, veal or chicken.

**CORIANDER** also known as pak chee, cilantro or chinese parsley; bright-green leafy herb with a pungent flavour. Both the stems and roots are used, so wash well before using. Also available ground or as seeds; these should not be substituted for fresh coriander as the tastes are completely different.

**COUSCOUS** a fine, grain-like cereal product made from a semolina dough, sieved then dehydrated to produce tiny even-sized pellets of couscous; it is rehydrated by steaming, or with the addition of a warm liquid, and swells to three or four times its original size.

**CRANBERRIES, DRIED** have the same slightly sour, succulent flavour as fresh cranberries. Available in health-food stores and most supermarkets.

**CREAM** we use fresh cream, also known as pure cream and pouring cream, unless otherwise stated.
**sour** a thick, cultured soured cream.
**thickened** a whipping cream.

**CUCUMBER**
**lebanese** short, slender and thin-skinned. Probably the most popular variety because of its tender, edible skin, tiny, yielding seeds, and sweet, fresh taste.
**telegraph** also known as the european or burpless cucumber; long (35cm and more) and slender, its thin dark-green skin has shallow ridges running down its length.

**CURRY PASTES** recipes in this book call for commercially prepared pastes of varying strengths and flavours. Use whichever one you feel suits your spice-level tolerance best.
**green** the hottest of the traditional Thai pastes; particularly good in chicken curries.
**laksa** generally medium in heat, laksa curry always contains coconut milk and rice stick noodles; goes best with seafood, tofu, vegetables and chicken.
**tandoori** a mild blend of tomato, ginger, garlic, paprika, lemon juice, onion and various spices blended with yogurt and used as a marinade.

**CURRY POWDER** a blend of ground spices, including dried chilli, cumin, cinnamon, coriander, fennel, mace, fenugreek, cardamom and turmeric. Can be mild or hot.

**FENNEL** also known as finocchio or anise; a pale green/white, firm, crisp, roundish vegetable about 8cm-12cm in diameter. The bulb has a slightly sweet, anise flavour, but the leaves have a much stronger taste. Also the name given to the dried seeds having a licorice flavour.

**FISH FILLETS, FIRM WHITE** blue eye, bream, flathead, swordfish, whiting, ling, jewfish, snapper or sea perch are all good choices. Check for any small pieces of bone in the fillets and use tweezers to remove them.

**FLOUR, SELF-RAISING** plain (all-purpose) flour sifted with baking powder in the proportion of 1 cup flour to 2 teaspoons baking powder.

**GAI LAN** also known as chinese broccoli, gai larn, kanah, gai lum and chinese kale; appreciated more for its stems than its coarse leaves.

**GINGER** also known as green or root ginger; the thick root of a tropical plant. **Pickled ginger** is sold in pieces or sliced, and comes in red and pink varieties packed in a seasoned brine.

**GNOCCHI** is the Italian name for a variety of dumpling. They may be made from potato, semolina, ordinary wheat flour, bread crumbs or a number of other ingredients, such as polenta.

**HARISSA** a Moroccan paste or sauce made from dried chillies, cumin, garlic, oil and caraway seeds. The paste, available in a tube, is very hot and should not be used in large amounts; bottled harissa sauce has less heat. Available from Middle-Eastern grocery stores and some supermarkets.

**HUMMUS** a Middle-Eastern salad or dip made from softened dried chickpeas, garlic, lemon juice and tahini (sesame seed paste); can be purchased, ready-made, from most delicatessens and supermarkets.

**KAFFIR LIME LEAVES** also known as bai magrood; the aromatic leaves of a citrus tree. Looks like two glossy dark green leaves joined end to end, forming a rounded hourglass shape. Used fresh or dried similarly to bay or curry leaves. A strip of fresh lime peel may be substituted for each kaffir lime leaf.

**KUMARA** the Polynesian name of an orange-fleshed sweet potato that is often confused with yam.

**LAMB**
**backstrap** (fillet) the larger fillet from a row of loin chops or cutlets.
**cutlets** small, tender rib chops.

**LEMON GRASS** a tall, clumping, lemon-smelling and -tasting, sharp-edged grass; the white lower part of the stem is chopped and used in Asian cooking.

**LEMON PEPPER SEASONING** a blend of crushed black pepper, lemon, herbs and spices. Available in most supermarkets.

**MESCLUN** a salad mix of assorted young lettuce and other green leaves, including baby spinach leaves, mizuna and curly endive.

**MIRIN** a champagne-coloured Japanese cooking wine; made of glutinous rice and alcohol and used expressly for cooking. Should not be confused with sake.

**MISO** Japan's famous bean paste made from fermented soya beans and rice, rye or barley. It varies in colour, texture and saltiness. It is a common ingredient in soups, sauces and dressings. Available from Asian food stores and major supermarkets.

**MIXED SALAD LEAVES** also sold as mixed baby leaves, salad mix, mesclun or gourmet salad mix; a mixture of assorted young lettuce and other green leaves.

**MOROCCAN SEASONING** available from most Middle-Eastern food stores, spice shops and major supermarkets. Turmeric, cinnamon and cumin add an authentic Moroccan flavouring to dishes.

**MUSTARD SEED OIL** rich and full-bodied with a buttery, nutty flavour, but without the heat or strong mustard taste. Cold-pressed oil is pressed from the whole seed, with no heat treatment, and is then filtered and bottled. It has a low saturated fat content and is high in omega-3 and monounsaturated fats.

## NOODLES
**bean thread** (wun sen) also known as cellophane or glass noodles because they are transparent when cooked. Made from mung bean paste; white in colour (not off-white like rice vermicelli), very delicate and fine. Available dried in various-sized bundles; soak to soften before using.

**hokkien** also known as stir-fry noodles; fresh wheat noodles resembling thick, yellow-brown spaghetti needing no pre-cooking before being used.

**rice vermicelli** also known as sen mee, mei fun or bee hoon; similar to bean threads, only longer and are made with rice flour instead of mung bean starch.

**PAPRIKA** a ground, dried, sweet red capsicum (bell pepper); there are many types available, including sweet, hot, mild and smoked.

## POTATOES
**baby new** also known as chats; not a separate variety, but an early harvest with very thin skin; good unpeeled.

**desiree** oval, smooth and pink-skinned with a waxy yellow flesh. Good in salads, boiled and roasted.

## RICE
**basmati** a white, fragrant long-grained rice. It should be washed several times before cooking.

**jasmine** fragrant long-grained rice; white rice can be substituted, but will not taste the same.

**long-grain** elongated grain, remains separate when cooked; most popular steaming rice in Asia.

**pre-cooked** is milled, completely cooked then dried. In its dried form, pre-cooked rice has a more porous and open appearance so that the boiling water can penetrate the grain and rehydrate it in a short time.

## SAUCES
**barbecue** a spicy, tomato-based sauce used to baste or as a condiment.

**cranberry** made from cranberries cooked in a sugar syrup.

**fish** also called nam pla or nuoc nam; made from pulverised salted fermented fish, most often anchovies. Has a pungent smell and strong taste, so use sparingly.

**hoisin** a thick, sweet and spicy Chinese paste made from salted fermented soya beans, onions and garlic.

**soy** made from fermented soya beans. Several variations are available in most supermarkets and Asian food stores. We use a mild Japanese variety in our recipes unless stated otherwise; possibly the best table soy and the one to choose if you only want one variety.

*kecap manis* a dark, thick, sweet soy sauce. The soy's sweetness is derived from the addition of either molasses or palm sugar when brewed.

*light soy* a thin, pale, salty-tasting sauce; used in dishes in which the natural colour is to be maintained. Not to be confused with salt-reduced or low-sodium soy sauces.

**sweet chilli** a mild, Thai-style sauce made from red chillies, sugar, garlic and vinegar.

**tomato** also known as ketchup or catsup; made from tomatoes, vinegar and spices.

**tomato pasta** made from a blend of tomatoes, herbs and spices.

**SILVER BEET** also known as swiss chard or blettes; may mistakenly be called spinach. A member of the beet family grown for its tasty green leaves and celery-like stems.

## SUGAR
**brown** extremely soft, finely granulated sugar retaining molasses for its colour and flavour. **Dark brown** is moist, with a distinctive rich, full flavour coming from natural molasses.

**caster** also known as superfine or finely granulated table sugar.

**icing** also known as confectioners' or powdered sugar; granulated sugar crushed together with a small amount of cornflour.

**palm** also known as nam tan pip, jawa, jaggery or gula melaka; made from the sap of the sugar palm tree. Light brown to black in colour and usually sold in rock-hard cakes. Substitute it with brown sugar if unavailable.

**white** a coarsely granulated table sugar, also known as crystal sugar.

**SULTANAS** dried grapes, also known as golden raisins.

**SUMAC** a purple-red, astringent spice ground from berries growing on shrubs that flourish wild around the Mediterranean; adds a tart, lemony flavour to food. Available from Middle-Eastern food stores and major supermarkets.

**TAHINI** sesame seed paste.

## VEAL
**cutlets** choice chop from the mid-loin (back) area.

**schnitzel** thinly sliced steak available crumbed or plain; we used plain (uncrumbed) schnitzel in our recipes.

## VINEGAR
**balsamic** originally from Modena, Italy, there are now many balsamic vinegars on the market; is a deep rich brown colour with a sweet and sour flavour.

**balsamic white vinegar** (condiment) is a clear, lighter version of balsamic vinegar; has a fresh, sweet, clean taste.

**cider** (apple cider) made from fermented apples.

**red wine** based on fermented red wine.

**white wine** made from a blend of white wines.

**WATERCRESS** also known as winter rocket. Is one of the cress family, a large group of peppery greens. Highly perishable, so must be used as soon as possible after purchase.

**WITLOF** (belgian endive) cigar-shaped, tightly packed heads with pale, yellow-green tips. Has a delicately bitter flavour. May be cooked or eaten raw.

**ZUCCHINI** also known as courgette; small, pale- or dark-green, yellow or white vegetable belonging to the squash family. Harvested when young, its edible flowers can be stuffed then deep-fried or oven-baked.

# conversion chart

## MEASURES

One Australian metric measuring cup holds approximately 250ml; one Australian metric tablespoon holds 20ml; one Australian metric teaspoon holds 5ml.

The difference between one country's measuring cups and another's is within a two- or three-teaspoon variance, and will not affect your cooking results. North America, New Zealand and the United Kingdom use a 15ml tablespoon.

All cup and spoon measurements are level. The most accurate way of measuring dry ingredients is to weigh them. When measuring liquids, use a clear glass or plastic jug with the metric markings.

We use large eggs with an average weight of 60g.

## DRY MEASURES

| METRIC | IMPERIAL |
|---|---|
| 15g | ½oz |
| 30g | 1oz |
| 60g | 2oz |
| 90g | 3oz |
| 125g | 4oz (¼lb) |
| 155g | 5oz |
| 185g | 6oz |
| 220g | 7oz |
| 250g | 8oz (½lb) |
| 280g | 9oz |
| 315g | 10oz |
| 345g | 11oz |
| 375g | 12oz (¾lb) |
| 410g | 13oz |
| 440g | 14oz |
| 470g | 15oz |
| 500g | 16oz (1lb) |
| 750g | 24oz (1½lb) |
| 1kg | 32oz (2lb) |

## LIQUID MEASURES

| METRIC | IMPERIAL |
|---|---|
| 30ml | 1 fluid oz |
| 60ml | 2 fluid oz |
| 100ml | 3 fluid oz |
| 125ml | 4 fluid oz |
| 150ml | 5 fluid oz |
| 190ml | 6 fluid oz |
| 250ml | 8 fluid oz |
| 300ml | 10 fluid oz |
| 500ml | 16 fluid oz |
| 600ml | 20 fluid oz |
| 1000ml (1 litre) | 1¾ pints |

## LENGTH MEASURES

| METRIC | IMPERIAL |
|---|---|
| 3mm | ⅛in |
| 6mm | ¼in |
| 1cm | ½in |
| 2cm | ¾in |
| 2.5cm | 1in |
| 5cm | 2in |
| 6cm | 2½in |
| 8cm | 3in |
| 10cm | 4in |
| 13cm | 5in |
| 15cm | 6in |
| 18cm | 7in |
| 20cm | 8in |
| 23cm | 9in |
| 25cm | 10in |
| 28cm | 11in |
| 30cm | 12in (1ft) |

## OVEN TEMPERATURES

The oven temperatures in this book are for conventional ovens; if you have a fan-forced oven, decrease the temperature by 10-20 degrees.

| | °C (CELSIUS) | °F (FAHRENHEIT) |
|---|---|---|
| Very slow | 120 | 250 |
| Slow | 150 | 300 |
| Moderately slow | 160 | 325 |
| Moderate | 180 | 350 |
| Moderately hot | 200 | 400 |
| Hot | 220 | 425 |
| Very hot | 240 | 475 |

The imperial measurements used in these recipes are approximate only. Measurements for cake pans are approximate only. Using same-shaped cake pans of a similar size should not affect the outcome of your baking. We measure the inside top of the cake pan to determine sizes.

# index

## A

almond coconut topping EV 105

apple and blackberry jellies FEV 113

apples, caramelised EV 103

## B

banana chillies with potato and green olive stuffing EV 46

banana split FE 110

beef

and eggplant bake with polenta crust E 8

and horseradish stew with kumara potato mash E 95

pasta bake with garlic and silver beet E 70

in black bean sauce with rice noodles and greens FE 20

stew with parsley dumplings E 96

bolognese E 70

chilli con carne with quesadillas FE 11

chow mein E 21

curried sausages E 24

meat pies E 12

mexican beans with sausages E 27

penne bolognese E 73

berry, almond and coconut slice EV 105

bread and butter pudding EV 102

burgers, lamb and burghul E 7

## C

cabbage rolls, pork E 99

cake(s)

honey spice sponge FV 107

rhubarb and coconut EV 112

caramelised apple tea cakes EV 103

capsicum, stuffed with pilaf EV 38

caramelised apple tea cakes EV 103

cauliflower, pea and paneer balti EV 94

chicken

stew, with chilli and tomato E 88

pilaf, with lentil and cauliflower FE 65

risotto, with pea and broad bean E 57

bake, with spinach and ricotta FE 78

patties, with tomato and fetta and spinach salad FE 16

chilli, with broccoli and cashews FE 20

creamy bake, with mushroom and asparagus E 77

green curry with meatballs E 84

jambalaya E 60

lemon grass curry E 98

spanish casserole E 93

thai red curry E 92

warm lentil and sausage salad E 26

chickpea, preserved lemon and risoni salad FEV 79

chickpea vegetable braise with cumin couscous EV 62

chilli chicken with broccoli and cashews FE 20

chilli con carne with quesadillas FE 11

chilli tomato sauce FE 18

choc-cherry microwave self-saucing pudding FEV 106

chocolate pavlovas, warm FV 113

clafoutis, plum FV 110

cottage pie, lentil EV 64

crêpes suzette V 100

curried sausages E 24

custard EV 102

## F

felafel FEV 58

## G

galettes, peach and walnut FEV 112

ginger sticky date pudding FV 111

gnocchi formaggio FEV 83

green curry with chicken meatballs F 84

## H

harira E 69

harissa braised vegetables with orange and mint couscous EV 86

honey spice sponge cake F 107

## I

irish lamb and barley stew E 89

italian braised sausages with beans FE 30

italian sausage and three-cheese lasagne E 28

## J

jambalaya E 60

japanese stir-fried pork with rice noodles FE 21

jellies, apple and blackberry FEV 113

## K

keema with chilli and tomato E 10

kofta, lamb, with chilli tomato and yogurt sauce FE 18

korma, lamb E 90

kumara potato mash EV 95

## L

lamb

irish stew, with barley E 89

keema with green chilli and tomato E 10

kofta with chilli tomato and yogurt sauce FE 18

burgers, with burghul E 7

korma E 90

moroccan tart E 4

posh sausage sambo E 32

rissoles with potato crush and rosemary gravy E 15

shepherd's pie E 17

spicy sausage pasta bake E 33

lasagne

italian sausage and three-cheese FE 28

roasted vegetable EV 40

lemon curd, blueberry and meringue trifle FV 104

lemon grass chicken curry E 98

lemon meringue pudding EV 108

lentil(s)

pilaf, with chicken and cauliflower FE 65

soup, with garlic and yogurt V 68

cottage pie EV 64

red curry FEV 54

warm salad, with sausage E 26

## M

meatloaf, prosciutto-wrapped pork and veal E 6

First Published in 2010 by ACP Magazines Ltd,
a division of PBL Media Pty Limited
54 Park St, Sydney
GPO Box 4088, Sydney, NSW 2001.
phone (02) 9282 8618; fax (02) 9267 9438
acpbooks@acpmagazines.com.au; www.acpbooks.com.au

ACP BOOKS
General Manager - Christine Whiston
Associate publisher - Seymour Cohen
Editor-in-Chief - Susan Tomnay
Creative Director - Hieu Chi Nguyen
Food Director - Pamela Clark

Published and Distributed in the United Kingdom by Octopus Publishing Group
Endeavour House
189 Shaftesbury Avenue
London WC2H 8JY
United Kingdom
phone (+44)(0)207 632 5400; fax (+44)(0)207 632 5405
info@octopus-publishing.co.uk;
www.octopusbooks.co.uk

Printed by Toppan Printing Co., China

International foreign language rights, Brian Cearnes, ACP Books bcearnes@acpmagazines.com.au

A catalogue record for this book is available from the British Library.
ISBN 978 1 86396 941 3
© ACP Magazines Ltd 2010
ABN 18 053 273 546